The Reluctant Spiritual Director

Fleetwood Range

WIPF & STOCK · Eugene, Oregon

Wipf and Stock Publishers
199 W 8th Ave, Suite 3
Eugene, OR 97401

The Reluctant Spiritual Director
A Handbook for Offering and Receiving Spiritual Direction
By Range, Fleetwood

ISBN 13: 978-1-60608-174-7
Publication date 10/14/2008
Previously published by Catacombs Press, 1996

Now this is eternal life: that they may know you, the only true God, and Jesus Christ, whom you have sent.

John 17:3

We have not received the spirit of the world but the Spirit who is from God, that we may understand what God has freely given us.

I Corinthians 2:12

If you discover a wise man, rise early to visit him; let your feet wear out his doorstep.

Ecclesiasticus 6:36

Acknowledgments

There are two persons who have been so important in the writing of this book that it would never have been produced without them. The first is my friend and benefactor, Ann Claire, who made it possible for me to receive the training that opened up my calling and led eventually to the writing of this little volume. The other is my self-giving and tireless soul friend, Jerry. She has encouraged me, pushed me, and blessed me in the writing. Then when it was done, she spent uncountable, frustrating hours with a computer, formatting my manuscript into the pages you see here. I am forever grateful to my Lord for the gift of both these friends.

WARNING!

HAZARDOUS MATERIAL!

It is essential to know that we are never to go into the inner journey without the **Lord Jesus**. **He** is our ultimate guide and spiritual director and will protect us from false voices and prideful error as we study and pray. This is so important that I urge you now, at the moment when you begin to read this book and think on these things of the inner self, to stop and ask the **Lord Jesus** to bless and protect you in your reading. If you happen to be standing in the aisle of a bookstore, don't let that deter you. Ask **Jesus** now to be with you even to the point of deciding whether or not to choose this book. It may be what **He** wants for you. But it may not. Ask **Him**. And listen. This is the first and most essential lesson for any and every spiritual director. Proceed with caution and all humility.

Contents

1 *Am I called to this ministry?* **1**
2 *What is a spiritual director supposed to do?* **13**
3 *The basic tools of the trade* **21**
4 *Other skills and helps* **39**
5 *How do I get these tools?* **49**
6 *What is a formal spiritual direction session like?* **57**
7 *Spiritual direction--informal* **71**
8 *Special considerations in working with women* **77**
9 *Areas of grace and special cautions in working with women* **89**
10 *How do I begin?* **101**

A Spiritual Director's Soul **107**

Annotated Bibliography **111**

The Art of Spiritual Direction **113**
Dreams **118**
Healing--Mind and Body **121**
Legal/Ethical Issues **123**
C. S. Lewis **124**
Living the Christian Faith **126**
Personality Types **129**
Prayer **131**
Psychology and Christianity **133**

1

Am I called to this ministry?

You haven't chosen this book and read this far out of idle curiosity. And you haven't continued in it to avoid boredom because few things are more boring than a discussion of the spiritual life for someone who does not desire it. I think it is safe to assume at this point that you have chosen this book either because you are being asked to do spiritual direction and are uncomfortable doing it or because you believe yourself to be called and are reluctant to accept that call as a true one for you.

There are several life situations that could call on you to do spiritual direction in spite of your disinclination. First, you may be ordained or preparing for ordination. If that is the case, people are going to come to you either for spiritual direction or for help with problems that are, at heart, spiritual problems. This work will inevitably come to you because of the very nature of the life you have chosen.

Second, you may be a professional counselor, trained to deal with problems through the lens of psychology, and find yourself more and more often faced with people who clearly need spiritual help. C. J. Jung observed in *Modern Man in Search of a Soul:*

> During the past thirty years, people from all the civilized countries of the earth have consulted me. I have treated many hundreds of patients, the larger number being Protestants, a small number Jews, and not more than five or six believing Catholics. Among all my patients in the second half of life--that is to say, over thirty-five--there has not been one whose problem in the last resort was not that of finding a religious outlook on life. It is safe to say that every one of them fell ill because he had lost that which the living religions of every age have given to their followers, and none of them has been really healed who did not regain his religious outlook.[1]

If you are a Christian and have been working as a counselor for 10-15 years, you will have experienced the truth of this and may be puzzled about how to deal with it.

Finally, you are quite likely to be a lay person wondering whether you are called to this ministry of spiritual direction. There are two equal and opposite traps for you as you work with this question.

The first trap is the more obvious one. In it you say, "I have intelligence, education, am a good Christian, and I like to help people. I would like to be a spiritual director." Such an approach involves both ignorance and pride. You feel both worthy and able, and you like the idea of being what you conceive a director to be. Pride is easy to see here. That doesn't mean you ***aren't*** suited to be a director. It may only mean you have a lot of work to do on the sin of pride.

The second trap is the reverse, mirror image of the first. In it you are humble:

It would be presumptuous of me to try to tell another soul how to know God . . .

I don't know enough . . .

I know people say I have helped them, but they don't know what they're talking about . . .

I know myself better than you do, and I'm not able . . not worthy . . . not smart enough . . . don't know anything about theology or the Bible . . .

Well, God's made a mistake if he's calling me. I know better . . .

Hear it? The "**I**" ringing throughout? This is **pride** speaking in its humble disguise. It is the appropriation to myself of the right to judge my own life. Wherein is the humility of handing my life, in all its sin and weakness, over to God? Of offering my frightened "yes" to His call? Of being willing to be a fool for God if that is how it turns out?

Pride is a chameleon.

The pride here is simply that ***I*** know better than God what ***I*** am capable of, and ***I*** do not trust God in this. Pride is a chameleon. It can masquerade as many things, but perhaps its most dangerous guise is this false humility. It looks like humility, sounds like humility, and talks like humility--but it is still pride.

I should note here that sometimes this same pride of unworthiness manifests itself in an acceptance of the calling coupled with a refusal to seek help for oneself. I remember one directee who was a conscientious, hard-working young priest. He described a killing schedule of counseling and directing in his work of recent months, and I asked him who was giving ***him*** emotional and spiritual support. His reply was that he just didn't need as much support as other people did. Surprised, I asked, *Do you know what that's called? I guess it's humility,* was his answer. *No*, I said, *I believe it's called pride.*

The effect was truly like a thunderbolt! The young priest sat back in his chair as though slapped. Then he lowered his head and was silent for a long space, two or three minutes. Finally, he looked up and said, *Wow! I really don't like that. It never occurred to me that it was pride to avoid help while I was giving it. This is going to take some thinking, and I don't like it.* He did, indeed, think and pray through this question and grew beautifully.

Still, how ***do*** I know I am called to be a director? Didn't we just say there is a terrible potential pride in saying I have decided to be a spiritual director? It is, indeed, a fearful thing to agree to minister to others. We do "work out (our) salvation with fear and trembling."[2] What else but this, my friend, is every single Christian called to do? The only relevant question is not, ***Am I called to minister?*** but rather, ***To what ministry am I called?*** And when the answer comes, we must heed it whether or not it is the thing we feel comfortable with. Often enough it will be distinctly uncomfortable.

Scripture
Reason
Tradition

What we need to do is ask and listen, seeking God's will in the matter. There is a way of doing this--a three-fold test applied by Christians from the earliest days of the Church. The faith and the lives of Christians have always been supported and bounded by this test--scripture, reason, and tradition. The primacy of this test has been particularly evident in Anglicanism through the centuries. Archbishop Carey says:

> . . . the Anglican way has been that of bringing to bear upon matters of truth the threefold criteria of Scripture, reason and tradition . . . let me make it clear that classic Anglicanism affirms the place of Scripture as the cornerstone of our way of doing theology. Reason then insures that we do not drift into an unthinking fundamentalism, and tradition prevents us cutting ourselves off from the past.[3]

Let's take these three supports out of the abstract and look at them in the light of the specific calling of a spiritual director.

Scripture

Does what you are considering, in all its requirements and consequences, conform to the message of the whole sweep of the Bible, telling us who God is and how God is?

In this case, we ask whether spiritual direction is a valid calling in itself, sanctioned by Biblical teaching. There are actually two parts to this question:

> *(1) **Does God truly expect us to grow in our spiritual life?***
>
> *(2) **If so, is it possible for another person to help us do that?***

The Bible, as it recounts from Genesis to Revelation the story of God's longing after his people, gives us many examples of people who grow in the spirit--Abraham, Moses, and Nicodemus, for instance. The Bible also tells of those who helped others to grow--the prophet Nathan for King David; Elijah for Elisha; Paul for Timothy, and Jesus for the apostles and all whom he touched. Paul put his own answer to this two-part question when he wrote to the Ephesians, "Speaking the truth in love, we will in all things grow up into him who is the head, that is, Christ."[4] It seems clear, then, the Bible teaches us that we are to grow up in the spirit and share what we learn with each other. The question yet to be addressed for you, the reluctant spiritual director, is: Am ***I*** growing, and am I ***able*** to share what I am learning? This defines the Biblical calling of the spiritual director.

Reason

Does the responsibility you will take on pass the test of reason in the light of Biblical validity and your own person and life?

In other words, are there indications in your daily life over a long period of time that this is a true calling for you? After establishing in your own mind the Biblical validity of spiritual direction as a discipline, the essential personal question is left--has God revealed to ***you*** a calling for this ministry?

This is when it is essential to sort out the false humility of, ***I'm not worthy,*** (Of course you're not!) from the true assessment of your experience. What in fact has been happening over the first half of life for you? Have there always been people who sought you out for counsel? Have you had the kind of deep relationships in which the deepest things of the soul are shared? Are you increasingly approached on the basis of your perceived spirituality and approachability, even by new acquaintances? And do you find a touching of souls and a peace of spirit in these encounters?

This quality of being a person sought out by others is the prime sign of a true calling to spiritual direction. Tilden Edwards, Director of the Shalem Institute for Spiritual Formation in Washington, D.C., says, "The *chief* criterion in our selection of participants has been to see whether others spontaneously seek out the person for spiritual counsel. This criterion can be met equally by laity, religious, and clergy."[5]

And Mary pondered in her heart . . .

You can reasonably apply this criterion to your own life by listening. Listen to what your friends tell you about yourself. You may be surprised each time you hear it. You may feel inadequate and unworthy. But you must listen to what they say. If you are told that your listening, your questions, your comments have been soul-changing for another person, then this is a truth to hear. Don't reject it, but rather take it into your heart and ponder it, just as Mary pondered over the events of Christ's birth. What do these things mean? "Let me read with open eyes the book my days are writing--and learn," says Dag Hammarskjold.[6] Ask yourself, ***If a friend told me these same things had happened to her, what would I see in it?*** We are so much more accepting of others' talents than of our own. Macrina Wiederkehr quotes this wise little prayer, "O God, help me to believe the truth about myself no matter how beautiful it is."[7]

Taken as a whole then, right now, how does your life ***feel*** to you? ***Read*** your life with care. Weed out both pride and false humility in this reading. What is left? Is there a core of truth you can acknowledge? What does your heart feel? (We thinkers have to be very careful here to ***feel*** with the heart instead of ***thinking*** with the mind.)

If there is a right feeling to the suggestion of spiritual direction, then bring your reason further into play and consider your preparation and/or possible further training in the discipline. Is this possible for you? Remember--if people are already coming to you for spiritual counsel, there is always room to learn more of this art.

Edwards speaks of a great need to raise up a new level of spiritual companion, one who falls between the "graced master and the gifted but unpolished friend." He says,

> Gifted friends, unnecessarily limited by lack of perspective and support . . . can end up providing others with an environment for first aid, when in fact they could be providing a fuller, deeper, more flexible long-term environment.[8]

Yes! And this is precisely why one who is called is obligated to respond.

Would you not send an emissary to a friend?

But the obligation is not all there is to it. God is not seeking children who will grit their teeth and do their duty. He is longing after the love of His children. If you are estranged from your child, do you not long to throw a bridge of love between you? Carrying out the trash is not the real issue with your teenager. Having him perceive the passion of your love for him is. If you had the chance, would you not send an emissary to an estranged friend? Would you not rejoice in a person who would help you regain your relationship with your loved one? This is what the loving Abba pleads with you to do when He asks you to guide the spiritual growth of another. Bring the soul He longs for to the Father in love, through the Son, by the guidance of the Holy Spirit. Listen together to the love song of your Lord.

You can learn much that will help you. This will be discussed at length in Chapters 3 and 4. You can certainly apply reason to your own experience. In the end, though, the best way to have confidence in your calling to spiritual direction is to be in direction yourself and test the idea thoroughly with your director. This, too, will be discussed in Chapter 4, and I urge you to follow this path if at all possible. Thomas Merton said truly that "books, lectures, and written instructions of past masters are no substitute for direct contact with a living teacher, who knows our innermost thoughts."[9]

Tradition

Does the change you will make in your life conform to the understanding of the Christian life expressed by the earliest Christians--those who knew Jesus Christ when he lived among us in the flesh?

Will you be abandoning another Christian responsibility to do this work? If, for instance, you have a young family dependent on your income and/or nurturing, and you are considering joining a religious order, there is a valid question as to which calling must be fulfilled first before God. You have to face and answer such questions, though the options are usually far more subtle than this.

The trick is to separate the true, continuing Christian responsibilities from neurotic attachments or already completed responsibilities. Exploring that question is, you will find, part of your growing in the spirit. One of the most straightforward ways of dealing with it is to picture yourself talking with Jesus face to face. If you tell Him what you plan to do, will He smile and bless you? Will He comfort and encourage you? If you ask with an open will, you will hear His answer in your heart. You will know if the kind of life you are proposing to live is pleasing to him, conforming to 2,000 years of Christian practice and belief.

Can you ever feel worthy? I hope not. Joseph Jones offers an instructive anecdote in The *Catholic Digest:*

> There is a story about a famous spiritual director who was approached by an old monk twice his age and renowned for holiness. When asked by the saintly old gentleman to give him spiritual direction, the young director said, "I am honored, but I can't!" The wise old monk answered, with a twinkle in his eye, "I know!" Both were aware of who the real director was--the Holy Spirit. They started out on the right foot.[10]

And when you come right down to it, whatever you decide after consulting scripture, reason, and tradition, your Lord will keep you safe if it is Him you seek. Most of us, when He speaks, deny that it is His voice we hear because we don't like what He says. Some few of us have it backwards--we deny hearing Him because we do like what He says but don't believe we should have what we want. Either way, in our human pride we are denying the voice and the commission of our Lord. You may need to relax about finding the "right" decision and simply give it a try in the name of Christ. An anonymous author of devotions observed that:

> The very act of wanting to know is already following Christ. The very self-doubt which makes us so suspicious of our own call can only happen because we think responding to Jesus' call is important. We want so for it to be Jesus; we're so afraid it's just us. And we long for a simple, unambiguous call.
>
> If we want to follow Christ, we will. We may sometimes mistake our own desires for God's will, but God will help us to know that and adjust our reality accordingly. One thing only is necessary: we need only ask Christ to call us and ask for the grace to follow, and we'll get it right eventually. In the end, Jesus' call is stronger and sweeter than our own selfish desires. We'll learn to recognize it. We'll get there.[11]

Endnotes

1. Carl G. Jung, Modern Man in Search of a Soul (New York: Harcourt, Brace and Company, 1933) 229.

2. Phillipians 2:12.

3. George L. Carey, "The Archbishop's Voice." The Anglican Digest (Transfiguration 1994) 62.

4. Ephesians 4:15.

5. Tilden Edwards, Spiritual Friend: Reclaiming the Gift of Spiritual Direction (New York/Ramsey: Paulist Press, 1980) 207.

6. Dag Hammarskjold, Markings (New York: Alfred A. Knopf, 1973), 131.

7. Macrina Wiederkehr, Embracing Your Memories: A Journey of Healing for Lent (St. Louis: Creative Communications for the Parish, 1988) 18.

8. Edwards, 205.

9. Edwards, 56.

10. Joseph R. Jones, "Do You Need a Spiritual Director?" The Catholic Digest (June 1988): 102

11. Forward Day by Day (Cincinnati: Forward Movement Publications, Lent 1994) Feb. 15 entry.

2

What is a spiritual director supposed to do?

The simplest definition of spiritual direction I can give you is this: I take your hand in love and walk with you for a space in your faith journey. That's it. And, like all things of profound value, it is deceptively simple. Many, many things fall out from this "simple" relationship. And there is undeniably much that can be learned to enhance its power. But, though the learning available may sometimes be complex, the relationship and its goal must never be. ***Director*** and ***directee*** are never more and never less than two souls searching for God.

Because I am holding your hand and I love you, I will work and sacrifice to hold you to the path when you step away or want to turn back. I will, in fact, direct you. You, of course, may choose to reject my direction. The difficult part is that you may be right in doing so.

Only and always a helper and companion

My job is to help you in finding the paths for your call and in discerning the validity of the call that is heard. But the director is always and only a helper and companion. Only the directee can know what is true in his or her own soul, and the directee alone must make the final discernments.

> We have not received the spirit of the world but the Spirit who is from God, that we may understand what God has freely given us.[1]

There is a sacred center I as director must not touch. In all of this, the only safety we can ever have together is in the Lord Jesus. Together we listen to him. And we will know. He has promised.

As unique souls, we must walk in the way God calls us

The calling of a spiritual director is not to admonish and/or approve another but to explore with that unique soul. The director must search with the directee through personal experience both past and present, must suggest and encourage and discern with the person, and help him or her walk a Christian walk in the way God calls that soul to do. The spiritual director is a spiritual companion, but one who can stand a little bit aside and see more clearly where the footprints are pointing. The director is a companion who has learned something of the territory, how the paths run, what to expect. But most of all, the director is one who is seeking to walk his or her own path and is willing to ***share*** the learnings of it. Since we are each of us unique, there is no one of us who does not have something unique--and therefore useful--in our faith journey to share with another soul.

Spiritual direction vs. counseling

Though the art of spiritual direction uses psychology and deals with the living of our lives, it differs in crucial ways from counseling. Pastoral counseling, in particular, may be fuzzily equated with spiritual direction. It should be noted that it is not at all out of order to have someone seeing a therapist and working with a spiritual director at the same time, as the two disciplines are neither identical nor antagonistic, but complementary. The differences lie in the areas of:

(1) the reason for which the relationship forms,
(2) the goal that is set,
(3) the means employed to reach that goal, and
(4) the helper's concept of his role in the work.

(I am indebted in this discussion to the work of Gerald May and the exposition of it by Tilden Edwards in *Spiritual Friend.)*

THE REASON FOR WHICH THE RELATIONSHIP FORMS

In counseling we find a person in crisis who is seeking help. In the grip of an emotional problem that has impinged on day-to-day life in some way--family crisis, professional failures, addictions, etc.--the client seeks a helper of some official standing and credentials, such as a clergy person, psychologist, or psychiatrist, to help in dealing with pressing problems. The emphasis here is on crisis management and problem solving. The relationship almost always grows out of a major crisis in the client's life, and when the crisis is over the relationship ends unless it can be reestablished on a new basis.

In spiritual direction, however, we find a soul, whatever its level of psychological health, that is in search of God. The directee has sought out the director because the soul feels a call to spiritual growth and a need for help in attempting it. He or she may very well have sensed some presence of God in this director that is a drawing force to others. The person may be coming in simple hope of finding help and direction. The relationship, then, is not necessarily one of crisis, though crisis is frequently the trigger that forces a person to face the immediate and personal need to grow spiritually. Whatever the impetus for forming the relationship, the emphasis is on a continuing opportunity for growth and a continuing relationship between the two persons.

THE GOAL THAT IS SET

Pastoral ***counseling,*** conceived in crisis, has a specific goal--to ease the crisis, to heal, guide, sustain, perhaps even help effect reconciliation in the crisis situation. These are goals that can be spelled out, recognized and achieved. And once they are achieved, a new reason for existence must be found if the relationship between counselor and counselee is to continue. The goal for a pastoral counselor with any given client is to work himself out of a job!

The goal in ***spiritual direction***, however, is always receding into the future because it is completely unattainable. Spiritual growth is a never-ending process, not an achievement. The goal in spiritual direction is a question of ***where*** and ***who*** rather than of ***what***. The where and the who are one and the same--the presence of God. The process is that of being and becoming in God. The goal is not so much for the individual to achieve any given level of spirituality but rather that this individual should press on daily and deeply, journeying into the heart of God.

THE MEANS EMPLOYED TO REACH THAT GOAL

The pastoral ***counselor***, faced with a person in crisis, will labor to work out a plan of action in response to that crisis. The counselor, searching through his knowledge, will carefully and consciously formulate a treatment plan and work through it with his counselee. Ultimately, their efforts are expected to resolve the crisis in some fitting way. The plan may involve anything from a long-delayed confrontation with an abusive parent to the simple act of cutting up credit cards. It is important to understand that either of these two actions, and an infinite array of others in between, can result from spiritual direction, but the ***means*** employed to bring them about will be different.

Formulate a treatment plan and work through it

How? The difference is in how the action is generated. In the pastoral counseling model, the counselor is responsible for thinking the problem through logically and proposing possible solutions to the client, giving support in their implementation. Ideally of course, the counselor will help the person to think his way through to proposing these solutions himself. But the counselor in either case is directive as to the ***result*** to be achieved.

Listening and praying

In dealing with a directee, however, a ***director*** will not be making plans. He will be listening for the word of God in this moment. He will be praying for the other person and opening himself and the whole relationship to be a vehicle of grace at every moment. The spiritual director is directive only in suggesting methods of exploration while the directee himself must choose, for only the directee can know when something has removed a stumbling stone on the way to a closer relationship with God.

To formulate these suggestions, the director draws on both training and experience as to different kinds of prayer, meditation, and worship patterns historically employed by seekers of God. He or she will also draw on personal experience in previous direction situations. But when the Holy Spirit is allowed to move in the relationship, surprising syntheses and impressions are generated. Fritz Kunkel says, "Not in the presence of a minister or a psychologist, but in the presence of God, things change completely."[2]

Measure your level of personal surprise

A good test of whether you are doing pastoral counseling or spiritual direction is to look at the level of personal surprise you feel at the comments and suggestions you make and the effects they have. If you are never surprised by what you propose to a directee, then you may be doing conscious counseling instead of intuitively conveying grace to the directee. The only test of success for the means of growth employed is to recognize spiritual deepening in the directee. There is no one experience or emotion that must be achieved in the course of spiritual direction. Every soul will walk a different path.

THE HELPER'S CONCEPT OF HIS ROLE IN THE WORK

Here lies a thin, thin line of distinction that will make all the difference in whether you are a counselor or a spiritual director. the ***counselor*** inevitably develops a personal stake in the ultimate outcome with his counselee. At the end of the relationship, he will feel that he has either succeeded or failed in healing/helping that person. He or she will have nurtured some vision in mind and heart of what the counselee will be when healed, freed, and out of crisis.

In terms of the goal that was set for their work together, the counselor will be able to measure outcome. And because of this, the counselor will inevitably see his or her own role as one of responsibility for making that desired outcome happen. The counselor will attempt, however subtly, to "make things happen" with and for the counselee. The need to do this, the way the counselor sees his own role, will affect the means employed with the counselee. It will also affect future similar relationships in terms of their formation and the goals set for them.

The ***spiritual director,*** on the other hand, sees himself as standing not in his own established will for the situation but seeking the will of God in it. He or she must guard against even having a preconceived picture of how things should go in the directee's life. The director most certainly must not attempt to "make things happen" in the outer world with or through his directee. The temptation is enormous, the more so as spiritual bonds form with this directee, but it must not be acted upon. The spiritual director offers various means and loving support to make things happen in the inner life of his directee, but what those things are and what actions they may lead to in the outer world are not his to direct. Those decisions come in response to diligently seeking the will of God and leaving the directee free to choose.

The only measure a director can put to any spiritual companionship is this: Is the directee growing in the Lord Jesus? Is he or she healing from a wounded, God-rejected/rejecting soul to a soul that finds its peace and power in God no matter what the outer world has done to it? This, the walk toward the Light for which we were all created, is the will of God and the only will a spiritual director can serve.

Endnotes

1. I Cor. 2:12.

2. Fritz Kunkel, Selected Writings, ed. John A. Sanford (New York: Paulist Press, 1984) 287.

3

The basic tools of the trade

At the risk of discouraging the reading of this chapter, I think it wise to begin with one of the wonderfully gentle, practical comments of Gerald May:

> It seems to me that anything that really needs to be understood about life has to be understood by the least sophisticated or intelligent of us--which means there probably isn't all that much that we really have to understand.[1]

This is a truth no Christian should forget, and it is fine encouragement for the faint-hearted. But beware taking it as license to be lazy or to do less than the best you are capable of.

With that understanding, let us look over the tools available to us. The tools of the trade in spiritual direction are those practices and learnings which teach the nature of God, one's own unique, personal nature, and the nature of human kind. The three basic tools, then, are:

1. Knowledge of scripture--learning the nature of God,

2. A life of prayer--learning one's own nature as a unique child of God,
3. A working familiarity with psychology--learning the nature of humankind.

Scripture--Learning the nature of God

In my experience, the first, most basic tool in spiritual direction is knowledge of scripture--the Word. All that is needed is found there. All that validates what you do as a spiritual director is to be found there. An easy, ingrained familiarity with the scriptures is your first tool in action and your first defense against error.

There are three principal ways in which a person can know the Bible. The first is through knowledge gained by familiarity--the ongoing process of having scripture read to you as a child; hearing it read and discussed in church; if you were very fortunate, hearing it read and discussed at home; or regular Bible reading on your own. In this kind of exposure to scripture, you become familiar with the stories and themes of the Bible.

The second way of knowing scripture is through knowledge gained by study and exegesis. You may have taken classes at college or in your church, studied on your own, completed a seminary extension course, obtained a seminary degree, or maybe you are a seminary student right now. In this sort of study, you learn about the history, setting, and languages of the Bible in addition to the content.

The third way to Biblical knowledge is the steady, daily reading of the scriptures over long years. This might be called "soaking" knowledge. This is the practice that brings you to a sure knowledge of Who the scriptures are about and gives you quiet confidence in the nature of God as he has revealed himself there.

If your family background leaves you lacking that first route to knowledge of the scriptures, or if you are simply aware that your Biblical knowledge is limited, the other two routes are open and beckoning for you. You have but to begin. Start to read the Bible every day. Follow whatever plan suits you best, but read it every day. Then take advantage of whatever courses or private study are available to you to learn more of the history and setting and language of the Bible. Buy a few basic books:

1. A good, usable translation of the Bible,
2. A concordance matched to that translation,
3. A dictionary of the Bible,
4. An atlas of the Bible,
5. A brief commentary on the Bible.

These will serve you well through a lifetime and may also whet your appetite for a more extensive study of scripture.

You will find that as your ease with scripture increases, you will relax more and more with your directees, and your confidence in what you are doing as a spiritual director will grow. The Bible will illuminate your joint walk toward the Light of God.

Prayer--Learning our nature as unique children of God

How, you probably ask yourself, does prayer connect with learning your own nature in the Lord? Isn't prayer a matter of talking with God, of asking for his help? The answer to that question is no, it isn't. At least, those aspects are not by any means a full description of prayer. It is not merely that. A treatise on prayer is not within the scope of this small book. However, many fine and helpful books have been written on the subject, and you will find some of them discussed in the annotated bibliography. I would particularly recommend Richard Foster's *Prayer*.

Ongoing conversation with God

Nevertheless, I think it important to establish here the basis on which I include prayer as a tool for spiritual direction and a means of self-knowing, so I will discuss the subject briefly from that standpoint. The fullest life of prayer is one in which your prayer is constant. As with a successful diet, you change your way of living when you move into constant prayer. Prayer, as an ongoing conversation with God, becomes your way of living. You begin to find that your prayer is more a state of being than a thing you do. You look, for instance, at the person in front of you in the Post Office line, and find yourself asking, *Lord, why does this woman look so sad and burdened?* And then you speak a silent blessing over her, praying the Lord to go with her and comfort her. Or you are faced with an unpleasant attack from someone close to you, and you ask in your heart, *Lord, what should I do? Defend myself? Keep silent? Tell her I love her but still can't agree on this issue? How can I be your person here?* This is constant prayer on the front lines.

Jesus Prayer

Other times you will be aware that there is a prayer running in the back of your mind. Many times a day I become aware that some form of the Jesus Prayer is rolling over and over through my mind. It is often nothing more than a little phrase of adoration and invocation--***Jesus, Lord, come.*** On occasion, though, the full Jesus Prayer keeps me from fragmenting under pressure--***Jesus Christ, Son of God, have mercy on me, a sinner.*** I remember one searing 6-week period when I was faced daily with a friend's towering grief, and my head rang with the silent prayer, *Jesus, help!* He did. Every minute of every pain-filled day. This, in fact, is when I learned to pray even while talking and listening.

And do not neglect music as prayer. The hymn tune that runs in your mind all day, the theme from Brahm's "Requiem"--these, too, are prayer and praise. Accept them and rejoice in them as such.

Pray for guidance of the Holy Spirit

When constant prayer becomes a way of life for you, you will find it easy to follow the injunction to pray constantly during a spiritual direction session. You really can listen carefully to your directee and pray for the guidance of the Holy Spirit at the same time. And you will receive that guidance in both enormous gulps and delicate, tiny drops of grace. Part of the joy in the spiritual life is in simply recognizing these unexpected and unexplainable graces for what they are.

For example, I prayed for one person, an older man whose life was plagued with great ugliness at the time, that he might be given some spiritual joy. I had envisioned various possible spiritual experiences that might offer him this joy, but never did I imagine the homely, action-filled event that did in fact lift his spirit and stay with him--he played an absolutely perfect game of tennis!

This middle-aged man who had been a semi-professional tennis player in his youth experienced again that physical and mental "high" of being absolutely whole and concentrated. As he put it, "On that day I could do no wrong." He experienced again what it means to be whole and free. That tennis match was and still is both a physical joy and a beautiful spiritual gift from the loving Father. The prayer that says we know God is doing for our loved ones "better things than we can desire or pray for" [2] speaks deepest truth.

Constant Prayer

This life of prayer, this constant learning to speak my heart, feel my fellows' hearts, and hear what God is saying in my life--these things bring me to a new knowledge of myself and my relationship with God. I truly come to know him as the transcendent God of creation and as the gentle Abba who longs for me to share love with Him.

In the same way, I come to know myself in the rawest ways because I am bringing my life to Jesus with such immediacy. I tell him spontaneously what I feel and what I want and what I think I need, praying over each instance as it arises. As a result, I come to know what I feel and want and need more truly than I have ever before let myself know these things. In presenting myself in constant prayer to God, I come to know myself in new, deep ways.

Pray Now

When prayer becomes constant in the way I have been describing, it also becomes much easier to pray aloud and to pray extemporaneously. Your prayer will become so flowing and natural that you can and will share it. When your directee says, "My mother is ill. Please put her on your prayer list," you can put a hand on her shoulder and say, *Let's pray together now*. And do it. Such a response is indescribably comforting and instructive for this worried soul.

Psychology--Learning the nature of humankind

The Bible is, of course, as much a revelation of human nature as of God's. The sometimes subtle, sometimes hard-edged messages of its stories leave us in no doubt of the fallenness of human nature and of all that means as we work our way through lives of sin and redemption. But, just as a concordance, an atlas, and a commentary can help us to understand God as he is revealed in the scriptures, so psychology can help us to understand ourselves as we are revealed there. Sadly, the misuse of this valuable tool has caused many Christians to dismiss it out of hand and thereby lose some of the gifts our Lord has given us for our nurture.

It is well here to consciously set aside whatever negative opinions you may bring to the subject of psychology. We all know someone who is steeped in psychology and yet is making a dreary muddle of his or her own life. We have all read or heard declarations that strike us as little short of ludicrous and yet are attributed in seriousness to a psychologist or psychiatrist. And sadly, we may also know people who have been hurt by the influence of a psychologist/psychiatrist or who have struggled with a therapist who had no sensitivity or patience with the Christian convictions of the client. Nevertheless, I ask you to suspend whatever resistance you may bring to this subject and consider the following.

Insofar as psychology is an open and honest study of the true nature of humankind, it is valid and useful to those who deal closely with their fellows. Insofar as the Christian brings personal knowledge of scripture and tradition to the study of psychology and immerses himself in prayer, it is valid and useful among Christians.

For instance, if I have a deep and clear understanding of the kind of personality I am dealing with, I can avoid many blind avenues in working with that person. If I have a grasp of the general patterns in which the human mind operates, I can move more easily through the experiences my directee and I share. And if I have some ability to recognize serious mental/emotional disturbance, I will be quicker to refer my directee to someone better trained than I to deal with such needs.

C. G. JUNG

Having said this, I must now say that I do not consider just any psychological position to be helpful. All that I write here is based on a general acceptance of the theories of Dr. Carl Jung. When I first read

Jung in college, I thought to myself that here was a psychologist who seemed to see people in a religious way. He was clearly not a Christian, but neither was he God-rejecting as I saw Freud and his followers to be. Jung had some sense of God. I thought that, perhaps, he even longed for Him.

Some sense of God

As an adult, I have studied much more deeply in Jung through the mediation of Christian teachers and spiritual directors, and I have found that many things learned there have been seminal in my learnings about the action of Christ in our lives.

To be more specific, Jung's understanding of how personality is formed and modified, his concepts of the relationship between the conscious and the unconscious mind, and his work on the great God-gifts residing in our dreams have been enormously helpful. In current language, these tools quite literally help me to know where a directee "is coming from." And I find nothing to oppose in Jung's idea of individuation, as it seems to give an answer to Paul's injunction to

> work out your salvation with fear and trembling, for it is God who works in you to will and to act according to his good purpose.[3]

The proviso I would add for anyone going into a study of Jung is this: Jung limits his understanding to a God who works only within the individual, and he sees this God as containing within himself the darkness Christians know as evil. Consequently, Jung's idea of God is that he is incarnate but not clearly transcendent; he is loving but not wholly good.

These understandings of God can never be acceptable to a Christian. Nevertheless, they do not invalidate Jung's tremendous achievement in describing the life and action of the human mind. It is the tragedy of this great man that he could never perceive the living, loving, personal God behind those processes.

May Sanford Kelsey

For these reasons, it is important to balance any reading of Jung by reading also the works of committed, orthodox Christians who follow his ideas about human nature but who have made other discernment concerning his ideas on the nature of God. Prominent among these are Gerald May, John Sanford, and Morton Kelsey. Some of their works appear in the annotated bibliography included in this volume.

PERSONALITY INVENTORIES

Myers-Briggs and Kiersey-Bates

Built upon the personality theories of Carl Jung is the system of particular personality types developed by Isabel Myers and Katheryn Briggs in their Myers-Briggs Type Indicator (MBTI) tool for identifying 16 different patterns of personal action. A more accessible version of this test for the general population is the Keirsey Temperament Sorter found in *Please Understand Me*, by David Keirsey and Marilyn Bates.

NOT AN ETERNAL LIMITATION

Here again, this is usable information for a spiritual director, but only if he or she has a solid grasp of what it means. There is a rich variety of explanations and applications for this work in available books, and they should be read. However, it takes time to assimilate the ideas embodied in the various types, and a director should have a reasonable grounding in them before attempting to apply them to others. He also needs to bear always in mind that no person should be seen as eternally limited to a particular type--life is more fluid than that, and God is more creative.

Smalley-Trent

A third concept of personality typing that is more immediately accessible than either the Myers-Briggs or the Keirsey-Bates is that of Dr. Gary Smalley and Dr. John Trent.[4] They sort types into the categories of four animals--lion, otter, golden retriever, and beaver. These are easily understandable and can be fun to use with either individuals or groups. In addition, Smalley and Trent are Christians and bring this commitment to bear in their work. However, knowing that some groups must avoid using religious material, they have developed secular presentations of their ideas as well as presentations that discuss the Christian applications of them.

KNOWLEDGE OF HUMAN NATURE

There's not much to be said about this because there is too much to be said about it. All the preceding comments concerning a knowledge of psychology certainly hold true. But more than that, there is an elementary feel for human nature, for how people work, that comes only from working with them, whether in spiritual direction or in house roofing. It is a practical skill that is developed on the job. What will enhance it, though, is a commitment to observe and prayerfully think about what is happening as you go through life.

This is not as simple as it sounds. It is hard work to stay alert to the meaning and nuance of the life flowing through and around you. Some people are far better equipped by nature than others to do this, but you would not have read this far if you were not already aware of a calling and a basic, if untrained, gift for such discernment. Tilden Edwards says in his fine book, *Spiritual Friend*:

> You do not have to be a psychologist, but you do need a basic sensitivity to the way human fears, yearnings, and experiences condition, if not determine, the way people respond in the

> group. For some people, such sensitivity is intuitive out of their general life experience, rather than something they need to learn. [5]

The important point is that both routes to such basic sensitivity, the intuitive and the nurtured, are valid.

It is deeply painful to look honestly at all that happens in and around your life, considering what your own part may be in it for good or for ill. In the end, it simply cannot be done without Jesus at your side to love, forgive, encourage and guide. Invite him to be there and ask for his help. You will learn more with time, and he will withhold you from doing any serious harm as you go.

HEALING OF MEMORIES

Read your Bible and Pray Constantly

Here again we have a tool of immeasurable value that is subject to deep suspicion. And there is no denying that it can be misused so as to be valueless or even to cause harm. But bear in mind that this is absolutely true of every grace given by God. Again and again I say, read your Bible and pray constantly. The loving Jesus will protect you and your directee if you allow him.

The spiritual practice of the healing of memories is based on the Christian understanding of time. Jesus was questioned about how human relations could be made right after the events had taken place (the question concerning the seven brothers who all married the same woman and died before her--Luke 20:27-40). His response was one even his questioners applauded:

> He is not the God of the dead, but of the living, for to him all are alive. Some of the teachers of the law responded, 'Well said, teacher!'[6]

In this exchange, Jesus shows us that God is the creator of time, not subject to it. Time is contained within eternity, and time will be consummated in the way of God's eternal purpose, not in the way of man's flawed living of it. Therefore, because he is the God of the living, Jesus can go into any time with us, past or present, and shed his love and grace on the events of that time. Leanne Payne quotes C.S. Lewis as saying, "All times are eternally present to God," and goes on to comment:

> He understood how the divine forgiveness, the eternal efficacy of the work Christ accomplished in Gethsemane and on the Cross, works all the way backward in time to the first man, Adam, and all the way forward to the last man who will ever be born . . . . By our repentance and the shedding of His Blood, Christ walks back in time as we know it, forgiving our sins and healing our sorrows, so that we may find wholeness.[7]

The key here is that **JESUS GOES WITH US.** The healing of memories is not meant to be some magical alteration of the lived past. Neither is it a psychological bandage to mask the pain of an old wound.

A healing of memories session would go much like this:

1. Director and directee will pray together and aloud for Jesus to be present in all that they do, think, and see in their work together.

JESUS PROTECTS YOU

2. The directee will then set the scene that is causing him so much pain, anger, or sadness. He will do this by any of several means--writing it in a journal, speaking it aloud while in a relaxed posture with eyes closed, or maybe letting the director lead him into the scene to the extent that he or she has been made aware of the facts.

3. Seeing the scene in his mind, the subject now asks Jesus to come into it--if the Lord has not already appeared in his heart's eye--and bring His love and grace to the event.

FACTS ARE NOT CHANGED

4. Directees will report many kinds of experiences in this living prayer. Often Jesus will simply comfort them with the knowledge that He was present when this thing happened, that He comforted and protected the person then, and that it is by His love that he or she has come through the experience. Sometimes Jesus will bring antagonists together to speak words of peace and love to each other. Again, He may hold the person in His arms and show him how the pain and sickness of the other person or of one's own self caused this terrible event, and this opens the door for the forgiveness that heals. This is not to say that the person may not express a great deal of anger and resentment along the way, but such an expression in this safe place is part of the healing.

5. Director and directee thank Jesus for being present to them in this work and ask Him to continue to bring forward in their hearts any other such memories He would have healed.

We believe as Christians that the healing we experience in this timeless time with Jesus is also experienced on some level by the other person or persons involved, living or dead. God's grace spreads throughout eternity and is not blocked by the barriers of already-lived time. It is a fact, difficult to believe but quickly known to the heart after having the experience, that such a healing of a memory will truly change the present. The directee will find he has drained the anger, lanced the festering boil, given up the wounded resentment, and can deal with the other person if he must and with his own life in general out of a new inner peace. This is a powerful means by which we can respond to Paul's admonition to "get rid of all bitterness, rage and anger, brawling and slander, along with every form of malice."[8]

The healing of memories does not change facts, but it does change feelings and perceptions, and this is where the pain is. To take a mild example, a child, denied the right to run out into a busy street, perceives only the limitation and perhaps even physical correction from his parents. His perception is painful and can be no other while it remains unexamined. But when, as an adult, he perceives the love that was truly operating in the event, he can begin to let go of the feelings of limitation and frustration. Most of us accomplish this kind of memory healing in the course of our adult lives, but what do we do with, say, our parents' divorce? Where are those feelings? And how are they still dictating to us 40 years later? In the spiritual exercise described above, it is never too late to take our pain to our parents and finally say all we felt and find comfort.

How can we trust the results of a healing of memories session? Might not the evil one slip in something that will be harmful to us or to others? This is why we pray so fervently for the presence of Jesus Christ. He will protect us. And the measure of the result is quite simple--is it loving? If it is not loving, it is not of God. James says,

> . . . the wisdom that comes from heaven is first of all pure; then peace-loving, considerate, submissive, full of mercy and good fruit, impartial and sincere.[9]

We can never overestimate the love Jesus has for us. We can never be sufficiently aware of his longing after us. But Jesus is, as St. Theresa said, "a gentleman." He will not force himself on us. He will not force his grace upon us. He stands meekly, humbly, but longing for us.

> Here I am! I stand at the door and knock. If anyone hears my voice and opens the door, I will come in and eat with him, and he with me.[10]

In the healing of memories, we are inviting him in. Archbishop William Temple, in commenting on this passage, said:

> He waits till we open the door of our hearts to let in His love which will call our love out. He never breaks down that door. He stands and knocks. And this is true not only of His first demand for admission to the mansion of the soul; it is true also of every room within that mansion.[11]

And so, as we move though the rooms/memories of our soul's mansion, we must each time invite Jesus in, and in doing so He will fill that room with His grace and love.

DREAMS

Gerald May says, "Sometimes even our dreams are prayers."[12] I believe this. God created us as creatures who dream. From Genesis to Revelation, the people of God ponder and respond to dreams.

Dreams are a way of knowing that was accepted by the fathers of our faith. Indeed, in large part our faith grew out of their responses to seminal dreams. Think of Joseph as a child and later as a slave in Egypt.[13] Remember Daniel giving his interpretation, and the warning implicit in it, to King Nebuchadnezzar.[14] And what of Joseph's role and that of the Magi in protecting the infant Christ and his mother Mary?[15] Pilate's wife, a pagan we suppose, "suffered much" in a dream because of Jesus.[16]

THE DREAMER MUST CHOOSE

I urge you to take the time right now to go back and read the relevant scripture passages mentioned above and reflect on how often these dreams referred to the dreamer's own attitudes and actions, warning of change that was needed and the dire consequences that might result without it. The choice always lay with the dreamer. Nebuchadnezzar paid no attention, little Joseph did not learn to curb his pride, Pilate ignored his wife. But Daniel understood and gave the king God's warning; Joseph took an enormous risk in marrying Mary, then joined the Magi in prudent action regarding Herod. The list of dreamers, their dreams, and their subsequent action extends throughout the pages of the Bible and deserves close attention.

I find it impossible to read these stories of the faith and deny that God uses this same method of speaking to us today. Below our veneer of civilization, we are creatures who dream. Science has demonstrated conclusively that if we are deprived of dreaming sleep, we will begin to break down mentally and lose touch with reality in a matter of days. This could only be true if this dreaming mechanism somehow assists the mind in sorting through and evaluating all the choices that have to be made in day-to-day life.

Share with a friend

The more we pray for Jesus to live in us, the more we are likely to dream. Then, what we need most is the desire and conscious commitment to remember our dreams. We can fall asleep praying for the presence of Jesus in our deep heart. When we wake, we can write down what we remember. We can then pray and ponder over it. A Christian companion or your spiritual director can often give you a different view of a dream. Indeed, dreams are so much a part of us that it is often quite difficult to see what may be blindingly obvious to someone else. Sharing your dreams with a trusted friend can be an exercise leading to much spiritual growth.

This is the simple, Biblical basis for including dream work in the art of spiritual direction. They are one way God speaks to us, and we ought not to lock the door on them. As for the multitudinous books, symbol dictionaries, and such on the market, you will need to select carefully, do a lot of personal testing of theories, and keep a light touch. For some suggestions, refer to the annotated bibliography with this volume.

****

A grasp of the principal insights of psychology will, indeed, make our progress together more fruitful as long as we remember that psychological health does not exhaust the meaning of Christianity. We seek Christ, and our own wholeness is only a means to that goal. Being "OK" will not work as the center of our life's target.

Psychology is not a religion; it is a tool. It is a tool for personal healing; finding personal healing is a means to a specific goal--Jesus Christ himself. Our goal is to find healing in Him so we can know Him in the fullest sense of the word. It is a far greater goal than improving self-esteem and feeling good!

Endnotes

1. Gerald M. May, Simply Sane: The Spirituality of Mental Health (New York: Crossroads, 1993) 163.

2. The Book of Common Prayer (Greenwich, Conn.: Seabury Press, 1928) 597.

3. Phil. 2:12-13.

4. Gary Smalley and John Trent, Love Is a Decision: Seminar Manual (Phoenix, AZ: Today's Family).

5. Tilden Edwards, Spiritual Friend: Reclaiming the Gift of Spiritual Direction (New York/Ramsey: Paulist Press, 1980) 191.

6. Luke 20:38-39.

7. Leanne Payne, Real Presence: The Christian Worldview of C.S. Lewis as Incarnational Reality (Wheaton, IL: Crossway Books, 1988) 75.

8. Ephesians 4:31.

9. James 3:17.

10. Rev. 3:20

11. The Anglican Digest (St. Louis, Lent 1994).

12. May, 156.

13. Genesis 37:1-11; 40; 41:1-40

14. Daniel 4.

15. Matthew 1:18-25; 2:10-15, 19-20.

16. Matthew 27:19.

4

Other skills and helps

A comfortable, free use of scripture and prayer, coupled with a wisdom about the workings of the human heart, are the basic tools of spiritual direction. There is no substitute for these tools discussed in Chapter 3 and no easy way to acquire them. Time, tears, and prayer form the pathway you must walk.

But there are other skills and helps which, building on these basic tools, can enrich both members of a spiritual friendship. These skills can expand the ministry of a person who has been limited to offering only the spiritual first aid of a gifted friend.[1] They can make it possible for this same gifted friend to offer rich new possibilities to others, teaching the helper to move from the superficial and speak to the deep hearts of these seekers.

This ability is crucial, for not infrequently the case is that a person who comes for spiritual direction also sets limits, consciously or unconsciously, and holds back. An unwary director will play into this. The flavor of the situation is like "$3 Worth of God."

> I would like to buy $3.00 worth of God, please--not enough to explode my soul or disturb my sleep, but enough to equal a cup of warm milk or a snooze in the sunshine.
>
> I don't want enough of God to make me love an enemy or pick beets with a migrant; I want ecstasy, not transformation; I want the warmth of the womb, not a new birth. I want a pound of the Eternal in a paper sack. I would like to buy $3.00 worth of God, please.[2]

This kind of reticence is usually present on an unconscious level in a new directee; occasionally it is quite conscious and actually expressed. This chapter will discuss the principal skills available to a director to help open these closed parts of a seeking soul. These skills are listening/silence, questions, feeling, trusting the Holy Spirit, and praying for others.

LISTENING/SILENCE

Listening and its flip side, silence, are, in my opinion, the centerpiece of skills. Listening involves silence as well as talk, and we are afraid of silence in our culture. C. S. Lewis refers to hell as the Kingdom of Noise! There is profound truth in this. Evil seeks always to confuse, and one way to do this is to crowd out the divine voice with noise. The poet Montale has said that the wish to huddle in groups, to create noise, and to escape from thought is a sign of desperation and despair. I believe this. Do not contribute your own noise to this evil work. Do not be afraid of silence. Pray in the silence. Be silent in the silence. Allow the directee to gather his thoughts, find his courage, feel his feelings in the silence. Let the

BE SILENT IN THE SILENCE

directee fill the silence with that which wells up in his or her heart. Pascal touched deep truth when he said that "all the unhappiness of men derives from one single thing, which is their inability to be at peace in a room." Allow peace and silence to open up before your directee when he is with you, and he will learn to walk into it when he is alone. He will find there the presence of God. The still small voice.

When your directee does speak into the silence, you must not only listen but be sure he or she knows that you are listening. This is a gift you can give every time you meet. It is a gift too rare in the rest of our days. It can, indeed, be a disorienting shock to someone who realizes he is truly being listened to. The person may actually resent this because more careful thought and choice of words is required when one knows that every word is heard and weighed. You may even be accused of "quibbling" about words.

Am I listening?

What made you feel heard? Did the other person turn fully to face you? Lean forward? Make definite eye contact and then return to that contact again and again as you spoke? Did your hearer's face respond with pleasure or pain or puzzlement at your story? All of these things are physical, body-language signs telling a person, "You are being heard!"

QUESTIONS

The right question at the right time--this is more truly an art than a skill; but, as with painting, you have to learn to handle the brushes and oils before you know what you are truly capable of in this area. Be assured that it is possible to be a very fine journeyman questioner and not necessary at all to be a Michelangelo-level questioner. The Holy Spirit can use whatever talent you have as long as you offer it all freely.

How will the directee know you are listening? Think about your own life experience. Perhaps there was a time when you were pleading your case to a professor, begging a treat from a parent, or maybe pouring out your heart to a loved friend. What things made you feel alone on those occasions? Did the other person look at the clock often? Shift his gaze restlessly around the room? Fidget in a chair or glance at papers? Did he or she avoid making eye contact with you? Stare blankly at you?

ASKING THE 'RIGHT' QUESTION

In Chapter 6, I will discuss the rudiments of a first session, detailing some questions I like to begin with. At this point, I want only to emphasize the nature of the questions you might ask. Your questions need to be thought-provoking and non-directive. If your directee pauses and puzzles before answering, you have struck a deeper chord in him and you will do well to remember what it was. Your questions need to open your directee to new perspectives, perhaps enabling him or her to step into a new area of thought. Your questions need also to provide you with any information that is vital to your understanding of the directee.

What your questions must not be are rhetorical (no answer possible), programmed (only one acceptable answer), accusatory (the old, "Have you stopped beating your wife?" variety), titillating to either of you, or born of sheer curiosity.

Your questions should show the directee that you care about him or her, that you are trying to get a clear picture of what you are being told, that you are **both** searching. Remember, too, that it is sometimes counterproductive to use glib, psychological wording that is familiar to a great many people in today's psychology-oriented world. If you repeatedly respond with something like the formula, "How do you feel about that?" the person may feel manipulated and become suspicious or secretive. Be creative. You will find this considerably easier to do if you are truly giving the directee a full dose of your listening gift.

Always look for the answer to this question: "Where is your pain?" But pray not to even think the question, "How can I fix you?" "Fixing" is not the work of a spiritual director. "Fixing" is the work of the Holy Spirit in the directee. Your job is to join in the search, support, and suggest possible paths.

FEELING

This may seem like an odd thing to list among skills and other helps. All people feel, don't they? Yes, but not all people know what they feel. To learn to know this is part of the maturing process in both day-to-day life and the spiritual life. Some people, and I have to count myself among them, have a great deal of difficulty getting in touch with what they feel. From the age of eight I learned to present an impassive front so as not to create any trouble in an already emotionally-charged atmosphere. The corollary of that impassive front was that I soon learned to simply not feel the grief, fear, panic, and anger I was hiding. To relearn that connection has been crucial to my spiritual development and to my work as a spiritual director.

GET IN TOUCH WITH YOUR FEELINGS

For example, if my directee tells me a story that is filled with her grief at the loss of a child, I can find my feelings of vicarious grief by putting myself in her place and my true feelings of fear by imagining the loss of one of my own beloved children. It is important for me to be aware of these feelings, perhaps even to express them to my directee, else she may stay miserably alone in her own grief. By feeling some of what she feels, I can share with her that which is deepest in her heart. I may even have a story of my own to give her.

And it is this kind of sharing that forms the bond of trust between two spiritual friends. You trust each other with your stories.

The value to me as director in being able to feel and share in this way is also great. In the Myers-Briggs personality typing scale, I am always an NT (an iNtuitive Thinker). This means, in effect, that I process things deep in the interior and apply rational thought processes to everything. If you ask me how I feel about something, I am likely to reply, "I think I'm angry about it." My own director will quickly come back with, "I didn't ask you what you think. What do you feel?" And it's hard for me to give a quick answer to that.

One excellent way I have found to enhance my feeling ability is the practice of Ignatian-type exercises. The general principal is to take a portion of scripture, read it several times, then imagine myself into the scene--either as a character or as an observer. I am very careful to see the scene in great detail, to feel the heat of the day or the ugliness of the crowd, and to feel the emotions of pity, fear, anger, joy that may arise. This gives me a sort of practice at touching my true feelings.

Beware in yourself and in your directee of denying that you feel a particular way or believing that you shouldn't feel a certain thing. You feel what you feel. What you do about what you feel is the issue between you and God and your fellows.

YOU FEEL WHAT YOU FEEL

Prayer, too, will help you to feel more. Time spent in the presence of God causes you to take on some of his love and compassion for his world. I have found that as my walk with Jesus intensifies, my eyes have begun to fill with tears when I watch the nightly news or read the morning paper. I have begun to grieve over the pain of the world just as I know he does, and this grief rises up in the presence of my directees as well as for unknown sufferers on another continent.

TRUSTING THE HOLY SPIRIT

Sounds simple, but it isn't! This can feel like pulling up to a trot in the middle of a race. The problem is that we inevitably think we see what needs to be done, and we want to make it happen. In my experience, trying to make things happen is the deadliest trap in interpersonal relationships. All the sad jokes about blind dates are witness to the danger of trying to make things happen between and for other people.

However much you may long to see your directee do or be a particular thing "for his own good," pray for the grace to keep your hands off his life. You can pray for him and with him, lead him in paths of thought he has not considered, but you cannot know what is best for him. Only he can know what is true for him and what is not when it it is time to make a decision in the presence of God. Support your directee in the process, but do not manipulate to achieve a particular outcome. Not in any way. Ever. Amen. You will be amazed at the ways God will choose for each individual soul, ways you never could have thought of.

PRAYING FOR OTHERS

I have already addressed the subject of prayer at some length in Chapter 3. I add prayer for others here as a skill because I have found it to be so. Prayer is active, concentrated, focused on the person. The soul for whom you pray is changed by your prayer--and so is your own. Your prayer has power to help the one for whom you pray, and it also has power to open and deepen your own being.

One of the clearest proofs of this is the simple expedient of praying regularly for someone who has the same problem you do. Alcoholics Anonymous and all of its spinoff, 12-step groups practice this principle in word and deed. They have found through long experience that the person who has lived it is best able to support another sufferer. Similarly, a woman who is agonizing over her faltering marriage will find that she grows in her own ability to cope with that as she prays for a friend at her office who is also experiencing marital problems. As with Elisha's message to Naaman, telling him to bathe in the Jordan to cure his leprosy,[3] this kind of prayer is so simple an assignment that we are disappointed and perhaps unwilling to perform it. But as Naaman's servant said to him, "If the prophet had told you to do some great thing, would you not have done it?"

So, do this. Pray for your own spiritual director and for all those who guide the souls of others. And teach your directees to do similarly with their life issues. There is no measure for this rich tool, for, as Gerald May says, "It is one of God's tricks on us that while prayer 'works,' we can't 'do' it that way."[4] We believe and we pray and we rejoice in what we see happen.

****

Spiritual directors need Spiritual Direction

There is, in addition to the skills just discussed, one other help that no spiritual director can do without. This is a spiritual director of one's own. This can be extremely difficult. You may be forced by circumstances of time and distance to have irregular meetings with your director. Once a month would be better, but no meetings at all will be deadening to the exercise of your calling. You are not a spiritual director because you have already arrived at some superior--and adequate!--level of holiness. You are a spiritual director because you are consciously on the path of spiritual growth yourself and have been given the gift and opportunity to share with others what you are learning. Meeting regularly with your own spiritual director accomplishes three things:

1. You will experience as a directee the effects of many of the same skills and learnings you use with your own directees,

2. You will be led to try more and different spiritual paths, increasing your heartfelt knowledge of what you may know only from books,

3. You will continue to grow in Christ. You must either grow or become cold; and if Christ is or becomes cold and distant for you, you cannot bring another soul to catch fire in him.

Endnotes

1. Tilden Edwards, Spiritual friend: Reclaiming the Gift of Spiritual Direction (New York/Ramsey: Paulist Press, 1980) 205-206.

2. W. Rees, "$3 Worth of God," The Anglican Digest (Transfiguration 1992): 29.

3. 2 Kings 5:1-15.

4. Gerald G. May, Simply Sane: The Spirituality of Mental Health (New York: Crossroad, 1993) 162.

5

How do I get these tools?

Let it be said clearly at the beginning of this chapter that there is no substitute for time and work. Inspiration comes after perspiration!

REGULAR SPIRITUAL DIRECTION

The tool that makes all the rest of them work is regular spiritual direction for yourself. This has already been discussed, but I bring it in again here because it is impossible to overemphasize its importance. It is often quite difficult to find a good director and adhere to a regular schedule. Find a way!

READING/STUDY

Reading is another valuable means of acquiring the tools of spiritual direction. Reading the ancient and modern classics concerning spiritual direction will help you immerse yourself in the subject sufficiently to make it an integral part of your thinking. Just as my fingers know where to go on this computer keyboard without my giving it a conscious thought, so the connections and insights of the spiritual director will begin to be a part of all you think, see, and do. It is internalized knowledge such as this that the Holy Spirit can bring to your conscious mind in the appropriate moments of your work.

To help you pursue a reading plan for your calling to spiritual direction, the bibliography for this text is divided into areas of interest--prayer, dreams, etc.--and is annotated. This list includes works not cited in the endnotes and is intended to provide a useful indication to the reader as to whether or not a particular book contains the kind of information and helps needed in any given instance. You will find that the same book may appear in more than one interest area, the reason for this being that it has valuable material in more than one area.

WORKSHOPS/RETREATS

There is an abundance of workshops available now for lay people and clergy alike. Some of these workshops and retreats are extremely helpful in learning the tools we have been discussing. Some, however, can be destructive sidetracks. You may have to go to some of them to find out. This is just one more situation in which it is crucial to have a good, regular program of personal spiritual direction, allowing you to measure the teachings of these workshops--and your responses to them--against the knowledge and experience of a competent director.

Be cautious of any teacher who puts himself or herself forward as a "special" focus of divine knowledge and/or who places any person or concept, including one's own self, as the proper center and focus of

BEWARE FALSE PROPHETS

life. Only Jesus Christ can stand in that place, and any teaching that points anywhere else as the final goal is to be rejected. On the other hand, any teaching that assists a soul in becoming more open to Jesus is to be given due consideration.

I am partial to workshops that allow for silent times and private or small-group work. These are most helpful to me, as I am a personality type that thinks best in quiet and alone. Others will be too extroverted to be comfortable for long in such situations, and they will respond better to other, more interactive formats.

I have also found it a very satisfying and enriching experience to attend lectures and teachings by the authors of books that have been particularly helpful to me. This will often take the learnings out of my head and intuition (which is where my personality type tries to keep things) and into my gut where they can be internalized and worked through on a feeling level as well as in the thinking mode that is so strong a part of my personality.

It is easy to see in these comments how knowledge of personality types can come into play in all areas of spiritual life--one's reading and the choosing of workshops and lectures being obvious examples here. I consciously push out from the limits of my own, natural type in order to broaden my understanding of myself and others.

Retreats might more properly be included in the section on having a spiritual director, as the need and benefits are quite similar. There are many retreat houses available around the country, most of them of moderate cost for a short stay--as little as 2 or 3 days. Usually there is the option of a guided or non-guided retreat. I always choose the guided option if it is available. A different director in a different setting can bring out hidden things in one's soul and guide it into new pathways.

SCHOOLS OF SPIRITUAL DIRECTION

There are also various schools of spiritual direction offered around the country. The one with which I am most familiar is the one offered by the Pecos Benedictine Abbey in Pecos, New Mexico. This program is open to members of all denominations and consists of 6 weeks in residence at the Abbey over a period of 14 months. There is an initial month in residence with a group of 40-50 students. Basic spiritual direction principles and skills are taught, and each of the 40-50 students will have a personal director. After 14 months of supervised field work and further study, the class returns for 2 more weeks in residence for additional teaching, evaluation of experience, and personal direction.

The Shalem Institute in Washington, D. C., offers instruction for spiritual directors. They, too, have residential programs, but they also offer local programs for people who live in that heavily-populated area.

There are also some short-course schools available. I have, for instance, assisted the Rev. John Price of Texas with the presentation of a School for Spiritual Direction offered by Bp. Ashby of the Episcopal Diocese of Western Kansas and funded by a grant from the Jessie B. DuPont Trust. We began with 5 days in residence, followed by three 3-day followup sessions over the ensuing year. This school was attended by both clergy and lay persons, and the participants have gone on to establish an ongoing group in their diocese for the teaching and practice of spiritual direction. This format or some variation of it, because of time and expense limitations, may be the direction future education in this area will take.

PRAYER AND SACRAMENTS

MORTAR FOR THE BRICKS

Prayer and the sacraments are the mortar that holds together all the bricks discussed above--spiritual direction, reading and study, and organized schools and workshops. Prayer and the sacraments are where we meet most closely the Christ we long for in seeking spiritual direction. When all has been learned and tried and done, it is the Holy Spirit moving in prayer and the sacraments who will bring us to Him whom we desire. As with the earliest Christians, we must devote ourselves "to the apostles' teaching, and to the fellowship, to the breaking of bread and to prayer."[1] This is the Way. We cannot direct anyone else in it if we do not walk it ourselves.

****

You acquire these tools by setting out to get them. They are developed equally as much through an alert desire for them as by study and instruction. You can learn the different forms of prayer and study theories about the operations of the human psyche for a lifetime, and you will learn a great deal. But until you look on your friends and colleagues with new eyes, praying over them and digging deep in your own heart in order to understand them, you will not possess these tools.

I read my Bible every day, following various plans for such regular readings. I can recite the books in order, find them readily, and generally know where to look up the stories I want to refer to. But the payoff on this knowledge comes when it combines with the skill of listening, and I suddenly know what passage I should give my directee for meditation.

Again, I know a fair bit about methods of engaging a person's unconscious with his conscious life. There are many exercises for this that are rewarding and even fun to do. But when, in a moment of shared pain, the idea for something a little different opens quickly in my own mind, I offer it to my directee and often experience the joy of seeing and sharing new insights with that soul. There are many times when I come out of a session and must quickly write down the process we followed because it was so valuable and so unexpected.

For example, when working with a man whose relationship with God was burdened by a deep sense of being "bad"--much like a naughty little boy--the idea came to me to have him do a number of unusual things. First, I had him make a list of all the things that made him a bad boy in his grandmother's eyes (she who had raised him). Then, I had him write another list of the things that made him a good boy in his own eyes. Afterward, we went over the lists together and emphasized repeatedly that the first list was someone else's idea of little Sammy, and the second list was Sammy's own knowledge of himself. Third, I had him write a letter to his long-dead grandmother. He volunteered to read it to me, and I found it a powerful expression of his sadness at being unacceptable to her and his sureness that he was living out his true and God-given self. He experienced that day the grace of forgiveness for his grandmother and the grace of knowing wholeness (holiness) in God.

Finally, knowing the man to be a personality type that has difficulty with organization and routine, I pledged him to read these two lists and the letter out loud in his prayer time every Monday night for two months. I further pledged that I myself would hold him in prayer for this purpose every Monday night for two months.

Because we were geographically separated and not in regular contact, I cannot say what effect this had over the ensuing time, but I do know that he left that particular session with an encouraged heart and some specific tools to use when he was alone again. The point of this story is not in what I did here but in the fact that a great deal of training and theory came to bear in practice in a way I would never have planned. This is what is meant by grace-full spiritual direction, and it is a joy to experience.

I recall another time when I sat listening to my directee, feeling frustrated and very much a fraud because I had no clue how to direct her in her spiritual impasse. I just couldn't figure out what the real problem was. Over and over again I simply said, "I don't know what the trouble is, but there is a block there somewhere. Something is keeping you from opening your soul to God and trusting him." I could only tell her to pray for the grace of knowing what this block was so it could be removed. It was a very unsatisfying session for me, and I suppose it was for her, too.

Months later, when I was again in the area, she came to me with great excitement, telling a story of much pain and sadness that had transpired since I last saw her. But she was glowing with a peace I had never seen in her because, while dealing with the difficulty that had arisen, she had remembered an enormous disappointment in a particular loved person that had occurred in her grade-school days. And she knew then, clearly and without question, that she had made a life decision not to love too much or trust too much from that day. Walking forward through the memories of her life with Jesus, she worked hard to change that early decision. The freedom of it was written on her face. The block was gone.

This is how the tools go together. You see the world differently. You often see what no one else sees, and you will suffer for that. The suffering goes with the grace. The suffering is a part of the grace, and it is more than worth it! Elizabeth Barrett Browning knew this when she wrote:

> Earth's crammed with heaven,
> And every common bush afire with God;
> But only he who sees takes off his shoes.
> The rest sit round it and pluck blackberries.[2]

Endnotes

1. Acts 2:42.

2. Elizabeth Barrett Browning. Aurora Leigh.

6

What is a formal spiritual direction session like?

The spiritual director finds that the practice of the calling occurs in two ways--formal and informal. In other words, sometimes the meeting has been planned for the express purpose of spiritual direction. Very often, though, it has not. As is the case with medical doctors, spiritual directors often find themselves at a party or on an airplane with a wounded, hurting person and must respond to that person's need on some level, however subtle. Such situations, however, will be addressed in Chapter 7. For our purposes here, we will assume a planned and, therefore, formal session of spiritual direction.

Scheduling

TIME OF DAY

Agree clearly on a specific time. Be sure it is a time when you will be free from interruption and able to be alert.

A SLAMMED DOOR WILL STAY SHUT!

It can be gut-wrenchingly difficult for a directee to work up to the point of sharing something from deep in the soul. To cut such a person off in mid-sentence to answer a door or telephone is to rob him or her of a hard-bought courage and perhaps slam a door that will stay closed for months--if it ever opens again! The directee in such a situation both loses courage and feels devalued. Use an answering machine, hang out a "Do not disturb" sign, but do not interrupt your directee to conduct other business. You may never know how deeply he or she has been counting on this time to lay down an old burden or ask a long-suppressed question.

Similarly, if you always get sleepy in the hour after lunch, don't schedule a session then. With the best will and care in the world, you may still doze off while someone spills out his soul to you. This is so wounding it is to be avoided at all costs. By the same token, if you are ill or greatly upset, reschedule the session and tell your directee frankly that you know you cannot give your total, prayer-filled attention under the circumstances. Be aware of and honest about your limitations.

LENGTH OF SESSION

SET TIME LIMITS

Recognizing that there will always be a need to follow the leading of the Holy Spirit in each individual case, your general rule should be to adhere to whatever time length you have scheduled. Each of you will be more comfortable with a known beginning and end to the day's work. Keep a readable and accurate clock in full view of the directee. Knowing that there is a limit on available time will often help reluctant or verbose persons to forge on to the point.

One hour is the standard amount of time to schedule for such sessions, and I have found it to be about right. Forty-five minutes makes it difficult to do any "winding up," while anything beyond an hour and a half tends to fall into repetition and cataloging.

DEPENDABILITY

Be there and be on time! When a person has spent the wee hours of the night before and the entire trip to your meeting place gathering the courage to broach a painful subject, a locked door and the quick suspicion that you have forgotten is killing to the action of the Holy Spirit. Never forget, never doubt, the level of joyful, if nervous, anticipation a directee can bring to a session of direction. "Do not put out the Spirit's fire."[1]

FREQUENCY

This will vary with circumstances, of course, but the important point is to always have the next session written on the calendar before your directee leaves. When the last thing a person says is, "I'll get back to you," chances are it won't happen. You schedule regularly to acknowledge the importance of the spiritual direction relationship and to give the directee the helping pressure of accountability. In another 2 weeks or 4, he or she will need to answer your question, "How has the new meditation approach worked for you?" And he will do the meditations if only because it is a certainty that the question will be asked. The operative theme in scheduling ahead in this manner is commitment!

COMMITMENT

How often? Even the least orderly of us are ordered to some extent by the clock and the calendar. Because of the way our year is put together, it is generally easier to schedule once a month rather than once every 3 weeks in ongoing spiritual direction relationships.

Timing will be a function of available time and of distance as much as of desire.

A GOLDEN TIME

On the other hand, sessions should be more frequent in the beginning of a spiritual direction relationship. It frequently happens that when the hole is punched in the dike of a person's psyche--when he or she is pressed to seek new depth in the spiritual walk--the contents will come spilling out so fast that even weekly sessions will barely suffice to handle it in the beginning. This is a golden time when some things may show up that will go back into hiding as the probing continues. You will be glad of the chance to know they are there for future work, so try to take full advantage of it.

First sessions, even with persons known to the director, should be scheduled for about two hours. This will give quiet time to begin knowing each other on a new, spiritual basis and also allow time for a Keirsey-Bates personality evaluation. Subsequent sessions should be the standard hour but perhaps scheduled only a week apart until three or four sessions have been experienced. It is at this point that director and directee can assess the relationship and address the issue of whether it would be a good thing to continue together. If the decision is to go on, then it is usually time to switch to a regular schedule of every 2-4 weeks.

Physical arrangement

You are going to welcome the directee into your heart, and you owe this person the hospitality of that new home. Make your guest comfortable. Within the bounds of possibility, don't have the room too hot or too cold. Don't offer a chair that is too hard, too soft, too big or too small. (The story of "Goldilocks and the Three Bears" has a point to make here!) Don't search around and try to make room as

though there isn't really a good place for an "extra" person to sit. This is admittedly a negative list, but the positive side is obvious without being specific. It's all well and good to say the directee's chair should be comfortable, but you must really be aware that a 5'1" woman is uncomfortable and psychologically reduced to childhood when her feet don't touch the floor!

Always keep a jug of water and a glass handy and offer them freely. However, if you wish to offer coffee or soft drinks, do so at the beginning of the session instead of suggesting a break to get such things. Hospitality can become intrusive on the session if you don't think ahead.

TRUE PRIVACY

We have already discussed the importance of arranging things so there will be no interruptions. Be equally sure there is true privacy. The directee should not have to worry about being overheard outside the room and should not be concerned that someone may walk through the area and see him or her. You do not want your directee to have any exterior reasons for holding back the true self.

Think about the kinds of things that occur in spiritual direction sessions and be prepared. For instance, more than one box of good tissues should be available in the event of either tears or a sneezing fit. A sturdy table, paper and pen should be available for each of you for making notes or drawing. A Bible should be at hand and a book of prayers. Any material you have thought to recommend to the directee should be available for inspection, as this will make the person more likely to follow up on a purchase if such is necessary. The point is to encourage them in acquiring new materials and to avoid spending their direction time in searching through your bookshelves for a particular book. Besides, when you have a stack of thoughtfully selected material for this directee's specific needs, he or she will be validated and encouraged in the effort to grow.

And don't neglect to make yourself comfortable. It is usually best to come out from behind the desk if you are in your office. However, if you are most comfortable in your desk chair, and the directee can sit beside the desk, there is no harm in your staying there. The important thing is to avoid placing the desk, a barrier and a symbol of superiority and authority, between you. It is usually best to sit so that you can easily look each other in the face (no glaring window light behind either, for instance) and close enough to be able to reach out and touch the hand or arm of the other person. Often, when emotion is high, a simple human touch will release the pent up feelings, but you do not want to distract or call attention to yourself by getting up and walking across the room. There are, of course, many cautions about proximity and touch, but these will be addressed elsewhere.

Finally, make your heart as ready as your room. Rejoice in the grace given to you in the entrusting of this soul to you if only for this one hour in all eternity. Treasure this person in your heart, thank God for him or her, and then give welcome to your meeting place.

First session

PRAYER

#1 RULE: PRAYER

The number one rule is to begin with prayer. You will have begun already with your private prayer, but now it is important to share prayer with the directee. But be careful. A long, rambling, personally intrusive prayer about the directee's particular situation is likely to be interpreted by him or her as being preached to. And it very likely is exactly that! A short prayer, either written or extemporaneous, asking God's blessing and the presence of Jesus in your time together, is all that is needed. It will be both a blessing and a reminder of your reason for coming together, for you do so in the name and presence of Jesus Christ.

Do not abandon prayer once you begin to talk. When you are puzzled or unable to think how to proceed or perhaps are moved by powerful feelings, ask Jesus to be with you and work through you. Do this consciously even as you listen to your directee. You may find it helps to keep the Jesus Prayer moving quietly through the back of your mind. This is a primary means of allowing the grace of God to come into the specific moment. This is often when you will hear yourself asking questions or making suggestions that will surprise you because they are so effective and yet you "don't know where they came from." They come from the Lord if you will remain open to Him.

CONTENT

Beginning questions

Experience will teach you better than any book how to begin with a given person, but it is always well to have some specific questions in mind to get started. The four questions I usually ask first, in this order, are:

How did your soul grow up? This is not a request for the story of the person's life but for his or her spiritual autobiography. How does this person see God having moved in his life up to this point?

What is your prayer like? Press for specifics. Be sure you have a practical knowledge of what this person does and feels in terms of his or her prayer. I once had a directee who confessed to being too uncomfortable to sit or kneel in prayer and so paced steadily up and down the room.

Though I did not necessarily think this was injurious, I suggested that the directee, who was quite large, try one of the desk-type chairs that distributes a person's weight in a partially sitting, partially kneeling position. Such a chair was available to this person at that time.

The result was most gratifying. The directee reported that it was possible to stay still and silent for considerable lengths of time when using this piece of furniture, and the receptive quality of the meditations did seem to change when the walking activity was suspended.

Who is Jesus for you? Press for complete honesty here. It is essential to know where on a scale that runs from "role model" to Lord of all" this person puts Jesus Christ. You know you are both headed toward knowing him as Lord, but the answer to this question tells you where your directee is on that road.

Why do you want spiritual direction? Why did you choose me? These questions are not always needed or even appropriate. Experience and judgment will tell you whether they need to be asked.

Personality work

TEST FOR TYPE

One of the excellent tools available to spiritual directors is the Keirsey Temperament Sorter. This little questionnaire, based on the Myers-Briggs theory of personality and temperament type, is found in *Please Understand Me* and may be administered by any lay person. It is short, easy to complete, and usually enjoyed by the directee. After the Sorter is taken and scored, you can give the directee a short introduction to the Myers-Briggs theory and an indication of what it may mean for him. It is useful to either loan the individual a copy of the book *Please Understand Me* or provide a sheet of descriptions covering his or her tested type. Be sure to keep note of the type for all your directees, as you will often find it relevant to your work with them.

Assignment and next meeting

SPECIFIC ASSIGNMENT

You may have already made several suggestions to the directee, but this is the time to go back over them. You will probably want to tell the person to choose among several assignments--to try a particular form of prayer, for instance, or to explore a significant dream event, or to meditate on a specific passage of scripture.

Make note of the assignment so you will know how you might begin in the next session. Making such an assignment and following up on it can be a strong impetus in the directee's journey toward God. Human nature is such that it responds to this challenge and feels consolation when the work is done. Your directee needs encouragement to go on.

Finally, try always to have the next session written on your calendar before the directee leaves. This, too, is an encouragement and an incentive. It has the pull of accountability, but even more deeply it has the support of caring. It says, ***This is important. You are important. I do care!***

Prayer

If the number one rule is to begin with prayer, the number two rule is to end with prayer. Praise God, give thanks for the movement of the Holy Spirit in this time between you, and ask the blessing of Jesus on each of you while absent from each other, promising that each will pray for the other daily. Send your directee away with your peace.

Subsequent sessions

PRAYER

This never changes. Always begin with prayer. Always continue to pray as you listen and speak. Always end with prayer.

CONTENT

Now the landscape opens up before you. Basically, you begin by following up on what has struck you most strongly about the previous session. If you have been in daily prayer for your directee and in intense prayer for him or her on the day of the appointment, the Holy Spirit will lead you to the area that needs attention. (There is much to be said about the director's formation in such prayer and discernment, but that is outside the scope of this book, and I refer you to the annotated bibliography in this volume.)

It will sometimes happen that the directee comes in with something new and pressing. By all means, pursue this. However, a wise director will check to see if this new development is an outgrowth of something initiated during the previous session. If so, the directee should be helped to make this connection and see the meaning in it. For example, if I have been praying with a woman over questions of secular vocation and she comes in upset about a dream of a young man who is bound and weeping, there is a direct, critical connection between the two. We will need to look at whether there are valuable masculine parts of her that are languishing and not being brought to God and used in her present work.

Perhaps, to use all the gifts God has given her, she needs to put aside her doubts and find a job that provides her with more individual responsibility and decision making. As St. Paul says, she is a particular part of Christ's body and must live that part for Christ.[2] If she does not, she will forever be seeking for the something that is missing, for "If one part suffers, every part suffers with it; if one part is honored, every part rejoices with it."[3]

SLOWLY IS THE KEY WORD

Additional areas of spirituality can be explored as the relationship grows. Dreams should be brought in right away since "presenting dreams" just before and after the first appointment will often indicate for the director a tone and area of emphasis for the early sessions (see Chapter 3). Slowly, checking always the fruit or lack of it from various disciplines attempted, you can go through dreams, forms of prayer, Bible study, healing of memories, and other means of growing in Christ. Slowly is the key word here. Give plenty of time for the attempt at a new discipline. Tilden Edwards warns, "In our cafeteria culture especially, there is the danger of running across the surface through many disciplines without giving any an opportunity really to assist...."[4] Go slowly, for you cannot be given direction as a director by other than the Holy Spirit. This is why a director is so greatly in need of his or her own director to aid in continuing personal formation and discernment.

SILENCE

A word needs to be said here about silence. There is another book to be written simply about silence and listening, but I want to emphasize that silence is a gift to be treasured and encouraged. I have already discussed in Chapter 4 the director's responsibility for allowing silence and using it in the course of a direction session. It is also worthwhile to begin work early with the directee, teaching him the need to create his own silence at other times.

Our society's tendency to overstimulate itself has become a pathetically effective means of blocking out the very spirit of God. We fill our ears with sound, our eyes with television pictures, and our minds with trivia and trash. When we are riding in our cars for hours and playing the radio or a tape every inch of the way, how can God speak to us in His still, small voice? When we sit almost catatonic in front of our television sets for 5 hours every day, how can we see the lovely things God longs to show us? How can we rest in God when we reside in noise and busyness? Bring these questions to bear for your directee and for yourself. We are all guilty.

How long, O Lord?

All relationships grow, change, and experience some form of death. This one will, too, and you must be sensitive to the life of it. You may need to refer the directee to a psychologist or physician in addition to working with you. You may also find that this person simply needs someone with different talents than yours. The relationship may be fruitful for two years and then reach a point beyond which neither of you seems able to pass. Discernment is critical here.

Sometimes all that is needed is a frank talk about needs, frustrations, and interests. You do not want to end a direction relationship simply because you perceive no movement in it. But you must not shrink from ending it when you believe another will take your directee on to new depths and heights in his or her walk with the Lord. And you must not bind a directee to you when the call comes to separate. Love him when he comes and love him when he goes.

Endnotes

1. I Thess. 5:19.

2. I Corinthians 12:12-31.

3. I Corinthians 12:26.

4. Tilden Edwards, *Spiritual Friend: Reclaiming the Gift of Spiritual Direction* (New York/Ramsey: Paulist Press, 1980) 161.

7

Spiritual direction--Informal

Since you picked this book up in the first place and have read this far, it is not unreasonable to assume that you are already functioning as a spiritual director. That's right. As was discussed more thoroughly in Chapter 1, you have realized that you are sought out by those who "need to talk to someone." You have humbly acknowledged that, as a regular pattern in your life, other people have found inner strength, wisdom, courage, and maybe even come to the Lord through you. The difference now is that you can name the experience--spiritual companionship/direction--and you can study and practice to do with more awareness and skill that which you have been doing.

This means that when you find yourself faced with any of myriad possible situations in which you hear another speaking to you from a searching soul, you will know how to pray and listen and be open to that soul in a new, more Christ-conscious way. While this expanded awareness can bring much blessing, it must always be held lightly in the knowledge that God may use you in these transient situations only if you do not allow the focus to move onto yourself.

"BARTENDER" ENCOUNTERS

One group of situations that may call for spiritual direction "on the hoof" are of the classic, "bartender" type. It is probably true that people tell their troubles to bartenders more often than to clergy or therapists. Alcohol artificially lowers our inhibitive barriers, and personal concerns and revelations may then pour out to any stranger who will listen. Unfortunately, and this should be borne in mind by anyone dealing with a person who is in the grip of alcohol, it also fuzzes the mind and the memory. You will probably hear clearly how the person feels, but there is no way to tell how accurate his story is, and he or she will likely have only the fuzziest memory afterward of anything that passes between the two of you. In short, a drunk can be assisted lovingly until such time as he or she is sober, but he is not a candidate for spiritual direction ***until*** he is sober.

THE QUICK-FIX MESSIAH

Similar situations, which may also involve alcohol-affected persons, are the strangers you meet on planes and trains and at parties. The temptation to be a quick-fix messiah can be subtle and irresistible. When the guy next to you starts to tell his story, you may be filled with a desire to be the person who "helps" him. Resist this with all your might. The director/companion who falls into the messiah complex can do immense harm to others and to himself. When you are accosted by strangers, keep in mind Paul's affirmation to the Corinthians:

> When I came to you, brothers, I did not come with eloquence or superior wisdom as I proclaimed to you the testimony about God. For I resolved to know nothing while I was with you except Jesus Christ and him crucified.[1]

Be Christ's Person

What you can be in these brief encounters is, quite simply, Christ's person. You can speak his name in quiet love as the one on whom you depend. You can suggest direction or therapy as may seem appropriate to the person. But understand that you are not there to "save" this stranger. Whatever God gives you for this soul, listen and pass it on quietly. God will grow the fruit, and you will most likely never know. Go on your way rejoicing and praising God, believing in his grace and power for this person.

LIMITED RELATIONSHIPS

Another sort of direction that is done "on the hoof" is that which occurs at retreats, workshops, and similar short-time gatherings. Here you are in a situation where there is time, opportunity, and intent for spiritual growth, and people are often touched powerfully by the Spirit as they listen, read and meditate. With the best will in the world, the leader or leaders of such events cannot serve as director to all the people who may need and desire such help. Participants naturally turn to each other--the roommate, the table mate, a discussion group member. And the person they choose may well be you, particularly if being so sought has been the pattern of your life (see Chapter 1). The need here is equally how to handle these encounters and to determine your responsibility in them.

1. First, of course, you must receive a request (which may not be made overtly) with tenderness. Anyone who seeks your counsel and tells his or her secrets to you is taking a risk that should be rewarded with gentleness and love.

2. Second, you must decide before the conversation goes deeper whether or not you have the resources at this moment to put aside your own needs for reflection and direction and instead enter into a relationship with this person. If, in fact, you are feeling needy and frustrated at

the interruption, at least ask if you can talk later. If you can't give yourself without being a martyr, ask to be excused at least for that moment.

3. Third, when you do get into the conversation, watch for indications that you are out of your depth. Experience is the primary teacher here, and you have to accept God's forgiveness for the mistakes that are inevitable. ***Remember that you can always listen.*** This is what is needed 95% of the time. If you offer no suggestions or analysis, you are not likely to do any harm. But if you listen with a fully engaged heart, you will sow peace in the heart of the other. Listen, pray in your heart, cultivate the art of the helpful question (see Chapter 4), and never fail to pray aloud with the person before you part.

4. Fourth, if as sometimes happens, the person who approaches you is deeply upset, ask for permission to call in help, then get a counselor, clergy person, or wise friend to come into the situation with you. If on the other hand, you have a fruitful exchange, you could offer to take the person as a directee if inclination and geographic proximity make that practical.

5. Finally, if this is a person you are not likely to meet again or will see only infrequently at similar gatherings, be clear about disengaging yourself from the relationship and referring him or her to professionals, other directors, or reading materials to pursue particular concerns. Again, resist the messiah temptation. It lurks in the heart of every spiritual director--the more so the more "successful" they appear to be.

REGULAR SMALL GROUP MEETINGS

This is a trickier area than the encounters with strangers described above. It is trickier because you feel and indeed have some ongoing obligation to the other members of a regular, small group meeting. It is tricky also because it is more difficult to defer or avoid altogether taking on the role of director in and for the group if they want to hand you that mantle. The challenge is to encourage the group to deal with each other as spiritual friends while discouraging them from becoming a problem-solving group for each other. The initial goals of the group--Bible study, healing, spiritual growth--should be pursued before any personal goals that may arise. And here is another challenge--keeping the needy person from taking over the group. Doing so is the responsibility of the leader, but you may have to help fend off such a person in order to save yourself.

In fact, if you are there only as a member of the group, there may be a point at which you have to state that in so many words. The messiah/guru complex appears in these situations and must be as vigorously opposed here as elsewhere. If it is allowed to take over, you will find yourself in conflict with group leaders and unable to profit from the support of a community of friends. It is a lonely thing for you to be always a chief and never an Indian. It is also unfaithful, for if you constantly gravitate to the center, the group will be deprived of other, varyingly talented leaders in its midst. You are not the only resource Christ has in that group. Never forget that! Leave room--lots of it.

Endnotes

1. I Corinthians 2:1-2.

8

Special Considerations in Working with Women

For the near future, until more lay people can be prepared for the work, most formal directors are likely to be men and most informal directors will probably be women. Also, since women as a group seem more willing to acknowledge a need for help and follow up by seeking it out, most directees are going to be women. It follows, then, that for the time being there will probably be a preponderance of relationships in which a man is acting as director for a woman.

NURTURING PROCESS

In addition to the obvious requirements of this situation, there is the fact that directing is a nurturing process. It requires the gift of a person's feminine nature. A male director who has not been able to nurture his feminine side is then--in addition to lacking personal wholeness--at a distinct disadvantage in dealing with anyone, but especially with the women who come to him for help on their own

spiritual paths. This impediment has to be acknowledged and addressed openly before such a person can be adequately equipped to follow the calling of spiritual direction. Let me add that a female director can also be more governed by her masculine self than by her feminine side and so be in equal need with the male director. I am indebted in much that I say here to the excellent work of Margaret Guenther in *Holy Listening*[1] and recommend her comments on this subject to all interested in pursuing the nurturing aspects of spiritual direction.

Physical arrangements

I want to reemphasize here some elements of the physical arrangements discussed in Chapter 6.

1. A woman may be more consciously sensitive to the feel of a place, and it is essential that the feeling be one of welcome, safety, and equality for her. At the same time, you will want to avoid any appearance of fussy perfection that is oppressive and potentially guilt-inducing. If you don't have a feel for this sort of thing, you surely know someone who does. You could ask a woman in whose home you find yourself feeling welcome and safe to make suggestions on how you might arrange your office or meeting place.

2. Have a good place to sit for everyone who comes to you. This includes small women. Don't make a small woman sit in a big, wingback chair with her feet dangling. It is not only uncomfortable for her, but it also makes her feel like a child. You don't have to buy a new chair. Get a footstool and have

some cushions available. Since women will frequently come to you laboring under some feelings of dependency and fear, don't encourage these negative factors by letting them feel physically small and insignificant.

3. Have more than one box of tissues easily available around the room so that getting one does not become a big production. Women generally cry more freely than men do, and this is a good thing. It is one of their great strengths. Refusal or inability to cry is a block you will not have to deal with nearly so much in women as you will in men. You can be thankful for that.

Particular areas of difficulty

There are a number of impediments to spiritual growth that cluster around gender. For women, this cluster includes issues of self-negation, self-trivializing, and "floating" shame.

SELF-NEGATION

LEARNED IN THE CRADLE

The attitude of self-negation is basic for women but not intrinsic. It is, in other words, learned in the cradle but not carried in the genes. I have no wish to go into the sociological and feminist arguments on this subject. This is not an area to which I feel called. Nevertheless, as a practical matter in the practice of spiritual direction, I must raise the issue because this is a spirit-wounding, inhibiting life stance that cries out for healing before there can be fullness of growth.

The essence of this self-negation among women, especially among women born prior to about 1960, is that we grew up defined in large part by what we were not. Principally, we knew that we were not male. And we knew that this was a negative fact. It was conveyed very early to our ears:

Don't you have any brothers?

You're the third daughter? I'll bet your folks were hoping for a boy!

Words spoken over a two-week old baby--***She'd be perfect if she were a boy.***

Who does your daddy play catch with?

And, if your name is at all ambivalent in gender, ***With a name like that, I guess your parents wanted a boy.*** (Too often, of course, this may be so.)

By the age of six, most little girls absorb the barely disguised message of such questions and comments. The message is clearly, ***Too bad you weren't a boy.*** And if hearing it wasn't enough, life soon taught us the truth of it.

MYTH--BOYS DON'T LIKE SMART GIRLS!

Again, things are changing now, but my own childhood in the 1940s and 1950s was filled with frustrations based on my gender--I couldn't earn money with a paper route because girls weren't allowed. I couldn't earn money mowing lawns because no one would hire a girl for such a project. I couldn't play in the newly-forming baseball little leagues because they were only for boys. And I certainly wasn't supposed to be at the top of my class. My own, dearly-loved grandmother told me repeatedly that if I would just hide my intelligence, the boys would like me better. If this sort of daily bombardment by friend and foe won't convince a little girl that she is out of luck just by virtue of being a female, I can't think what would!

WE REJECT OURSELVES

The result of this deep belief that we are not quite what we should have been is a skewing of attitudes and priorities for women. Cosmetics, clothes, and diets are all means of making ourselves "better," more acceptable. And that includes being more acceptable to ourselves. We reject ourselves--the very selves Jesus loved and died for. And this is the point of wounding to be addressed by the spiritual director. It is the director's responsibility to lead this woman to accept herself as fully as her Lord does and to order her life in light of that acceptance. William Temple says:

> The world as we live in it is like a shop window in which some mischievous person has got in overnight and shifted all the price labels round so that the cheap things have high price labels on them and the really precious things are priced low.[2]

Women, especially women born before 1960 have grown up looking into that disarranged shop window and paying the false prices even while hating and rejecting them.

One of the skewed high prices a woman pays is in her body. She may become more concerned with making her body acceptable (e.g. diets, cosmetics, clothes) than with taking loving care of it. A simple example of this would be the lifetime of foot and back pain we acquire from wearing high heels. For another, it was a moment of real epiphany for me when I realized that I was sitting on a beautiful Caribbean beach for the first time in my life and was hesitating to swim in that delicious water because it would mess up my hair! God allowed me to see the foolishness of it while I was still there, and I am thankful to say that I swam. I also went home and had my hair cut off rather than continue to be a slave to it.

This may seem quite trivial to a man. If so, he needs to think it through until he feels the impact in its core reality. In the beach experience, I consciously took loving care of my body and soul by swimming in that beautiful setting. I have never forgotten the pleasure of it. And I also consciously set aside the value of being physically attractive; in particular, I set aside the value of being attractive at a level that was unrealistic and unneeded. I no longer needed or wanted to be remembered as the best-looking woman in the room but, rather, I wanted to be simply the woman who had luxuriated in that wonderful water. It was a freeing moment that stands out in my life's journey, and many things followed from it.

UNCONSCIOUS GNOSTICISM

Understand that women do truly carry this deep belief that they are physically inadequate and must make up for it, usually in some time-consuming, expensive, and even painful way. (Have you ever plucked your eyebrows or shaved your legs, gentlemen?) This belief leads them into a natural and unconscious sort of Gnosticism. Women can come to believe that their physical bodies are bad and their spiritual selves must be good to make up for it. This slips easily into the general Gnostic heresy that says all created matter is bad and only spiritual matters are good. And in a woman who neglects the nurture of her spirit, there is a double wounding because she is left with only her unacceptable body to carry her through life. It is not enough.

SELF-TRIVIALIZING

This may seem like another leaf from the same book as self-negating, and the two are certainly related. However, you will not have to search long through your memory to find a woman who, though self-negating in her life stance, is anything but self-trivializing in her behavior. Women who allow the angry, suppressed, masculine side of their natures to take control can be anything but self-trivializing! With them you will meet the rage of a lifetime head-on.

The self-trivializing woman, however, has a way of speaking and behaving that will not be so obvious. She will speak in a little voice, using little words, and treat her thoughts as little thoughts. She will drop her deepest ideas and feelings into a conversation in an offhand way, carefully keeping an escape door open behind her. For example, she may say something like this:

> **I thought afterwards that I should have told Mom how hurt I was...(pause)...but that wouldn't have been the Christian thing to do...(pause)...would it?...(pause)... Anyway, I got over it, and we're good friends now.**

There are basic questions of psychology, social interaction, Christian living, and discernment here. Your directee wants answers to them but does not have the personal confidence to ask them. Instead, she sets a scene, backs away from it, and hopes you will take her seriously. She doesn't commit to secure the answers because she isn't sure she has the right or perhaps even the knowledge to ask the right questions. Having been made to feel inadequate so many times in her life, she has learned how to avoid situations in which it might happen again. In this example, she phrases her thoughts in a vague and rambling way to which the listener cannot easily respond with some version of, "Wow, that is one stupid question, lady!" There is no real question stated. She protects herself and can hide behind the belief that what she said so offhandedly really wasn't very important.

LITTLE VOICE
LITTLE WORDS
LITTLE THOUGHTS

Rule #1--Be alert to what a woman trivializes. This material is not trivial for her. By the same token, be alert for what she does not say. If, for instance, she tells you a tale that calls for anger but never says she felt or feels that anger, pay very close attention. There is more to be known and dealt with here. Ask her gently. Don't put words into her mouth, but ask her where it hurts. The anger will show up; and when it does, forgiveness for the person who hurt her becomes a possibility. This is how a spiritual director can lead.

A self-trivializing woman will not be able to accept a compliment. She responds to compliments with anxiety. This anxiety can come from self-negation: "This isn't true about me, and I can't allow it to be believed." It can also come from a hard or danger-filled life: "What does he or she want from me?" In both cases, the woman does not believe the compliment is a true statement about her. In the first, she believes the speaker is mistaken. In the latter case, she cannot even believe the speaker is sincere. You will need to be sensitive to this stance because it can defeat a clumsy and obvious attempt on your part to affirm and build up the person without regard to whether or not praise is truly due.

Rule #2--Do not offer affirmations/compliments that are not sincere and deeply felt by you. She will know the difference, and you will damage the trust you are trying to build up. I have read somewhere this excellent affirmation from Rabbi Kushner:

> God not only forgives our failures; he sees successes where no one else does, not even we ourselves. Only God can give us credit for angry words we did not speak, temptations we resisted, patience and gentleness little noticed and long forgotten by those around us. Such good deeds are never wasted and not forgotten, because God gives them a measure of eternity.[3]

This is not blessing the trivial but finding blessing in the everyday. Going further back in Christian history for a similar affirmation, there is no parallel for the humble, joyful service of Brother Lawrence in his kitchen with the pots and pans.[4]

The psychological problems of self-trivializing are fairly clear. The spiritual backlash of it may not be so obvious, but it is devastating to spiritual growth. A woman who cannot accept a compliment has an even more difficult time accepting love, most especially the unconditional and unearned love God wants to give her.

Here is another place where the aspects of psychological health and spiritual health are hardly distinguishable. Such a woman cannot accept God's love. She does not love herself. And for that reason, the notion of loving one's neighbor as one's self becomes meaningless, if not frightening. Your responsibility as her director is to lead her into a new understanding of the primary Christian truth that our personal value is given to us by the loving God who created us. Nothing we are and nothing we can ever do will earn that love. We are simply loved because we exist and can rejoice in that forever. In God's love, no one is negated or trivialized.

UNEARNED LOVE

I should add here that this difficulty of believing in and accepting God's freely-given love for each of us, his children, is by no means confined to women. Though it may proceed from quite different roots, I have seen it often in men. One big difference to be aware of is that it tends to show up in men as a false self-confidence ("I don't need anybody!") and in women as a false humility (the inability to accept compliments and love, for example).

In fact, the most dramatic reversal I ever saw of this was in a man who was also a minister. There came a day when we talked about this in the morning, and he came back in the afternoon, face ablaze with joy, and told me--and anyone else who would listen--that while puzzling over it in prayer he had finally understood! He understood in his heart that he was completely loved by God for no reason at all except that he existed. It is not possible to describe the joy, the release from bondage, he showed that

day. And however many times the strength of his new conviction may have been tested since then, I have no doubt that he has been able to reach back and touch that hour of that day as the time when he finally knew it was true. Many, many women are looking for this same blessing.

FLOATING SHAME

It has been said that "guilt is the loneliest experience of which we are capable."[5] This comment applies well to the condition of many women if we change that first word - make it "shame" rather than guilt. Guilt is a feeling based on reality. It is tied to specific, actual deeds or omissions and can be healed by action -- confession and restitution, for example. Shame, on the other hand, may arise from one or a series of real events, but it leaps to an unsupported conclusion about ultimate self-value. Shame is, then, an erroneous life position that no amount of good works can erase.

Be assured that women are experts at feeling this negative life position of shame, and this may be part of the explanation for the loneliness that haunts so many of them no matter what their status in life. For many a woman, shame begins at birth simply because she is not a boy. She is the wrong kind of child. She perceives that she is not good enough in her most basic being, and nothing she will ever do can change that. But she keeps trying all the same. Doomed to failure in this most basic area of self, she is doomed to carry a heavy load of shame into her life. In such cases, unless the issue of gender adequacy is addressed, this unfocused, floating sort of shame will poison the springs of her soul.

A women is unlikely to express this problem by saying, " Gee, I feel so ashamed of being female." Indeed, she may stridently proclaim the very opposite. But this secret belief deep inside about herself may still exist and fester. Her deep inner feeling of being apologetic for her gender can then attach itself to anything in her life that is less than perfect - her hair, her hip size, her children's grades, her job performance, or her education.

Somehow this endless list of things that are not perfect becomes a list of things for which she is both responsible and answerable. And she has this ready pool of floating gender-shame to attach to it. That's the trap a women can grow up in or fall into unsuspectingly during a crisis in her life. It is there somewhere for every women, even for the one who is strong and confident appearing. Watch for the signs.

Endnotes

1. Margaret Guenther, Holy Listening (Cambridge/Boston: Cowley Publications, 1992).

2. The Anglican Digest (St. Louis, Pentecost 1994).

3. Rabbi Kushner. Specific source unknown.

4. Lawrence, Brother. The Practice of the Presence of God (Orleans, MS: Paraclete Press, 1985).

5. Forward Day by Day. Cincinnati: Forward Movement Publications, May-July 1994, 84.

9

Areas of grace and special cautions in working with women

Just as there are particular areas of difficulty for women, there are particular areas of grace. These are so valuable, so grace-filled, that you will do well to be keenly aware of them and capitalize on them in your work together.

THE NEED TO BE KNOWN

LONELINESS OF SOUL

When a woman reaches the point at which she desires spiritual direction, she is also quite likely to have achieved a conscious knowledge of her own deep need to be known. Men, I think, are more likely to come into direction seeking knowledge. They want to know. Women, however, often live in a wrenching loneliness of soul, feeling that their essential self is utterly unknown even by those closest to them. Worse still, they may perceive that there is no desire on the part of these others to know them in such a deep way.

The woman does not necessarily object to the roles by which she is known, but she begins to understand that she is much more than those roles and recognizes a need to be known in her true depth. The greatest loneliness for me has never been one of location or situation but has occurred when I was not allowed to share the joys and sorrows of my deepest heart with another human being.

The spiritual director here needs to lead a woman through this ***need*** to be known and into an open ***willingness*** to be known. It is from this seed that the flower of humility can unfold. But it is not enough to ***want*** to be known. Being known requires deep, painful self-disclosure, and such self-disclosure is an act of the ***will***. When a woman is willing to place herself before God - warts, bad hair and all- she can finally offer her full self to Him, accepting his unearned, grace-full love. With nothing left to hide and love still given, she is finally free--free to grow, free to live, free to flower.

My own experience early in spiritual direction may be illustrative of this. I had been in direction for about a year with a spirit-filled priest who had led me gently into new understandings of "the kingdom within."[1] He lived a long distance from me, which kept our contact minimal, and another possible director had recently moved into an area much closer. At the same time, I experienced through a close friend an inexpressibly painful event that required me to spend an intense period of weeks in an assisting role. As these things so often happen, I had been opened up, slammed with painful reality, and now needed help to sort through the experience.

I talked with the new person about a possible direction relationship, but since distance was still a factor, we had not made a definite date to get started. The Holy Spirit intervened. At a conference at which both I and my potential new director were present, I awoke on the final day with a dream which clearly pointed out my deep need to be known in my deepest self and sent me running to make that first appointment . Here is the dream, with some omissions for the sake of brevity and clarity:

> In the dream I was present at the very conference center where I was in fact sleeping that night. While talking with others, I saw a little child come into the room. He was very filthy, and I was horrified to realize that he was mine. I had neglected him, but apparently he had not been cared for by any one else either. I was horrified and guilt-stricken because he was my own child, and I knew him so little that I wouldn't have been able to recognize him if I had to pick him out of a crowd. When I tried to hold him and clean him up, he was bitterly defiant. He said it was too late and it didn't matter what my problems had been; he said I couldn't make him do anything and he would cause me great misery. He ended by saying, ***You'll never be able to clean this mess up!***

A PRESENTING DREAM

> But I loved him. And in desperation I grabbed him up and ran to the main room of the conference center to find my new director and ask him to help me with the filthy, awful little fellow.

Needless to say, I grabbed up this dream, ran to find my new director, and made the long-deferred appointment to begin. Anyone with a passing study of dreams will see what a wealth of material there is here. The point I want to make, though, is that this "presentation dream" at the beginning of the direction relationship announced with chilling clarity that the unknown, neglected parts of my soul and life were crying out to be known and healed. The shock of this dream left me open and willing to do this kind of painful, personal work. This is not an uncommon beginning with the women you will see seeking direction. Rejoice in it.

GENUINE CARING AND INVOLVEMENT

Women do get involved with others, especially other women. And they really, truly do care about each other. In the latter years of my own life now, I see and relish the fine thread of caring spun out from friend to friend across the years. It forms a network of relationship that is rich and full. Some friends are no longer in close touch; but should we meet, there is always that deep connection that lets us take up just as we were when we met last, even if that meeting was some 30 years ago. This is the kind of experience in relationship you will often find in a woman who comes for direction, and it will ease her path into a closer relationship with her Lord. She understands much of the giving and receiving involved.

MAKE EYE CONTACT

What is essential, then, is that she should feel in you a similar involvement with her. One way to convey such involvement is through eye contact. Women deal with children and understand the importance of eye contact in being heard and understood. Try, then, to engage in good eye contact with a woman as you speak and listen to each other. This will help her to trust you, and you will discover how much depth of knowing can come in this way.

The flip side of so much good connection with others is the possibility that a woman will talk too much or with too many others about a current problem or concern. I am most emphatically not raising an issue of gossip or idle talk here. I am talking about true sharing among friends. It has, however, been my experience that too much discussion of a problem with persons other than the director or counselor involved will dissipate the energy the directee needs to deal with the person and/or the issue she is working on.

It is similar to my own finding that when I am writing, I must guard against explaining my work in progress to another person. The thoughts and words I labor to express in such a conversation do not stay with me and somehow drain the quiet pool of thought inside. In other words, if I tell you what I am writing, I am rendered unable to write it. Similarly, if you talk a concern in three different ways to as many people, you may fail to act in a deeper, quieter confrontation with yourself. You may also grasp at easy answers offered by friends who want to help so much that they do harm by interfering. The kind of intentional reticence I am suggesting requires much discipline for a naturally extroverted woman--the E (extrovert) of the MBTI scale--but such discipline will allow the strengthening of her inner confidence and resolve. The dividends are great.

ABILITY TO EXPRESS EMOTION

Women are believed by many to be uniformly subject to broad emotional displays. Let me say that this is by no means true of all women. It certainly is not true of me. I am a thinker and have to make a thinking decision to let my emotions out. With work, I have learned to do this much more freely than I was able to do in earlier years. No doubt my friends and acquaintances would still say that I present a very cool exterior most of the time. The point here, however, is that the impediment to expressing emotion for me and women like me is compounded of both basic personality and some earlier experience.

Men, on the other hand, are always impeded to some extent by the injunction of our culture that manly men do not cry or show pain or fear. You will see this particular barrier far less frequently among the women you work with, and you can rejoice in this, too.

GIFT OF TEARS

Crying, as with silence, needs to be allowed. If a woman starts to cry, don't panic and look for a way to get her to stop. It is a prospering thing, not a harming one. Crying may be the way through a terrible door for her. Let her walk through it. Cleansed by the tears, she will be better able to tell you--to know for herself, for that matter--what she saw and heard and felt in the moment that brought the tears. Your response at this point is never, "Don't cry." It must be, "Why did you cry? What did you think when you cried? What did you see? How did you feel?"

Remember, though, that while tears are a highway to the inner spirit, they can be used as a defense. A woman who cries easily may quite unconsciously be using her tears as a hiding place. Experience has taught her that when she cries, others will stop pushing her and scurry to make things all right. Other persons may become frightened, angered, perhaps even judged by her tears. Whatever the reason, they want the crying to stop and will abandon the field to make that happen. Don't fall into this trap. Let tears run their course when they come. Be sympathetic and caring in your personal presence, but practice the art of silence and see what will come out of it.

TEARS MAY BE A DEFENSE

Special cautions

FOCUS ON ACCEPTING FEELINGS

With both women and men, but particularly with women, it can often be more productive to ask, "Where do you hurt?" than "How do you feel?" You will find that women, more often than men, will follow a deeply felt statement with such words as, "I shouldn't say that" or "I shouldn't feel that way." As I cautioned earlier, beware in yourself and in your directee of denying that you feel a particular way or of believing that you shouldn't feel a certain thing. You feel what you feel. God knows what you feel, and I, as your director, am certainly not going to faint at the revelation.

Ask her, "Whom can you offend by admitting this feeling to me and to yourself?" Try to lead her into an understanding that what she does about what she feels is the issue between her and God and her fellows. Sometimes you can defuse these "I shoulds" and "I shouldn'ts" just by having her say them very clearly out loud. There are many things that seem true when whirling in the brain and yet betray their falsity when spoken aloud for another ear to hear. You can listen for such ideas welling up in the words of women and help them to accept their feelings while learning new and more useful ways of responding to them. You can teach your directee to offer these feelings to God in prayer, growing through them.

A long-time friend once told me that the most helpful thing I had ever said to her was that though she did have to look after her grandmother and be kind to her, she wasn't required to like the manipulative, demanding old woman. Once she could stop feeling guilty for not liking an unlikable relative, she was more free to minister to her and better able to determine what was appropriate help. In the end, she even developed some sympathy for this grandmother who was entangled in a lifetime of angry loneliness. This in turn gave her insight into some of the difficulties of her own parent who had been raised by this woman. But without the simple acceptance of the fact that she didn't like her grandmother, my friend would probably have missed these other insights and the growth they brought.

FOCUS ON GOD'S UNCONDITIONAL LOVE AND FORGIVENESS

Lead your directee into an understanding that this love from God is not a negative sort of action in which he loves us "in spite of" who we are. Rather, it is a positive, affirming, "because of" love. He loves us because of who we really are, who he created us to be. He delights in us and longs after us. There is a renewal song that says, "God danced the day you were born." The full verse is:

You are loved, you are beautiful, you are gift of God, His own creation,
You are gift to all mankind, His gift of love to them,
You are loved, God danced the day you were born.[2]

Though the song may not appeal to traditionalists, it nevertheless expresses succinctly the feel of what it means to say--that God delights in us as his perfect creation. He sees us as we truly are, infinitely better than we can see ourselves, and he loves us. To understand this is to understand that there is absolutely no earning such love, neither is there any losing of it. I have often been moved to tears by the image of Jesus sorrowing over Jerusalem when he spoke these words:

> O Jerusalem, Jerusalem, you who kill the prophets and stone those sent to you, how often I have longed to gather your children together, as a hen gathers her chicks under her wings, but you were not willing.[3]

This is an excellent passage for meditation in coming to understand the poignant, longing love of God for his people. This is an understanding that women may have a particular need to grow into. When a woman can accept this unconditional love, then accepting Christ's forgiveness becomes possible for her, and that forgiveness will be related to real acts and omissions rather than to vague feelings and free-floating shame.

FOCUS ON HER UNIQUENESS

This concept is found at the center of the focus on God's unconditional love. Here the understanding to be sought is that the person God delights in is a one-and-only. As the old song says, "There will never, ever be another you." When your true self is not allowed to live, or when you are physically dead, there are particular things that will never happen, particular loves that will never be expressed, no matter how long time and the universe may roll on. You are the only bearer God has provided for these particular things .

For example, the child whose mother dies when she is three may have the most loving and nurturing of adoptive mothers, but the fact remains that the primary, visceral connection of birth mother and child is broken for a lifetime. That particular, unique relationship cannot ever exist for this child. Let me hasten to say that this is not meant to downgrade the adoptive relationship in any way. It is merely to observe that here is one possibility that can never be realized, though we know that God in his love and mercy will supply the need amply in other ways through other persons. Nevertheless, the plain fact is that if you are removed from your family situation by death, there can never be another you to fill your place.

This uniqueness of each child of God, the special place he or she occupies in the vast tapestry of creation, is a critical understanding for your directee. It is the creating hand of God that gives each of us our personal value, and that value is far greater than we can understand. This is why we give our lives back to the Lord and ask him to be with us in every minute. For a self-negating woman, knowing this one thing in her heart--that her value comes from God, lavishly given--is to step into an entirely new spiritual life. Someone has written that the sum of the universe itself is added to by the existence of an unpublished manuscript in an attic trunk. Such an understanding gives value and power to our smallest words and deeds.

CREATING HAND OF GOD

SOCIAL RELATIONSHIPS WITH DIRECTEES

It saddens me to have to include these caveats, but the world we live in calls for them. You must be cautious of physical contact and of social relationship with any directee, whether of the same or the opposite sex. This is because physical contact can lead to misunderstanding and even lawsuits, while social relationship can break down the objective distancing a director needs to employ.

I cannot tell you never to touch the other person, for there will be times when you simply must offer a reassuring hand or a comforting touch. There are moments when it would be unkind and unfaithful to do less. Nevertheless, such touching must be done with conscious care. It is one thing to touch a woman's hand or forearm briefly by way of offering comfort or connecting with a crucial idea. It is quite another to look forward to the times when you might do this. She will know the difference instinctively, and you must not blind yourself to it.

Be vigilant, then, against any personal desire on your part to touch this person. Be equally vigilant against any desire on the part of this person to be touched by you. These are feelings you must admit to yourself, and to your spiritual director, and to God and then exercise extreme circumspection regarding them. By using thoughtful, prayerful care in this area, you can avoid giving a false impression when you are merely being kind or a true impression when you really are struggling with some feelings for the other person. Do not be a stumbling block in the path of your directee in his or her walk with the Lord. Always remind yourself that this adventure is not about you.

DO NOT BE A STUMBLING BLOCK

Friendships with directees are both possible and probable. The realities of our lives are that a person may be in close association with the one who is his or her director--a fellow parishioner or perhaps the rector of the parish. The problem lies in the fact that as you grow closer in friendship, you each lose valuable objectivity toward the other and toward the relationship you share. As an example, a directee may gradually become less frank with you if she fears she will hurt you by being so. Or she may hesitate to admit anger toward a mutual acquaintance who is close to you.

By the same token, your direction meetings may become more of a mutual sharing than a directing experience. This may, in fact, be the direction you need to take, and a new director may be called for. These are things too personal to make rules about. It is more useful to follow this two-point method:

1. Get clear in your mind what the direction/goal of this relationship is,

2. Be diligent in asking the Holy Spirit in prayer to show you the way you are to follow in pursuit of that goal.

As always, when you have examined your heart, investigated the facts, and prayed deeply for guidance, you will not be far from the kingdom, whether or not you can recognize it as such at the time.

Endnotes

1. John A. Sanford, The Kingdom Within Rev. ed. (San Francisco: Harper & Row, 1987).

2. Origin unknown.

3. Matthew 23:37.

10

How do I begin?

There will come a point when you feel it is time to begin--a time when you can say, and need to say, "I am a spiritual director." You will probably already be involved in some spiritual direction relationships because you are a person to whom others come. But how do you offer yourself to the wider community? You are wondering, "How will I begin?"

The truest answer is that you won't--God will. He will push you to begin, and he will urge people to come to you as directees. But there needs to be a conscious moment when you acknowledge your new role and accept it--a time when you tell God you are ready and offer yourself to Him in this ministry.

For me, that moment came when I was attending the School for Spiritual Directors. One day I climbed the cliff behind the Abbey, sat on my favorite rock, feet dangling in the air above the river valley, and accepted this calling as my own. I did it out loud and in specific terms. I told Jesus that I would do this, that I knew he had given me the gifts I needed and was asking it of me. I also told him that I was afraid of what it would mean for my life, afraid of my pride, and all-in-all overjoyed to be called to something I so love doing. It was an intensely honest prayer in which I understood myself better than at any previous time.

This sounds deceptively simple, but it involved the overcoming of a wall of false humility/pride. I still find it difficult to say to someone, "I am a spiritual director." Either I am washed with shame at saying something so presumptuous (enter the false humility/pride again!) or I am scurrying to explain that this is not a version of Madame Olga's palm reading operation! I am never quite comfortable with giving myself the title of spiritual director. I pray that I never will be. Then the pride will have won for sure!

This sort of commitment experience may come to you within the context of your own spiritual direction. If not, you will need to talk with your director in very specific terms about your beginning to work as a director yourself. Tell your director that you feel ready and want to be commissioned in whatever way seems appropriate to the two of you. You may want to do the same with your priest or pastor, but this will vary with the particular local circumstances and attitudes.

Physical location and circumstances of time will have a lot to do with how many directees appear for you. I happen to live in a small city that is at an awkward distance for easy commuting with the large city nearby. Therefore, I know people who have expressed an interest in working with me, but the mechanics are difficult on any regular basis. I also do some teaching weekends and workshops introducing spiritual direction and do direction with individuals in the

GOD'S WILL IN GOD'S TIME

course of them. Some people I may see only twice a year. This is frustrating to my sense of order, but it is the way my physical location dictates things, and I have to assume that the Lord is doing with me what he wants done. It will be the same for you--different from what you imagine and always changing. Be loose!

The English have a saying that one should always "begin as one means to go on." I like that. It means that I must not lower my standards for myself or anyone else just because I am new at this. It means that I need to keep a spiritual director for myself from the very beginning, that I must carefully maintain a life of prayer and study, and that I should be as gentle and loving to myself as I am to others.

When you begin acting as a director, you may find that your relationship with your own director changes to one more of friendship based on equality than the director/directee relationship you began with. This is not a bad thing so long as you are still able to humbly submit yourself to direction and your director is comfortable with continuing. If, however, you become too good friends, then you may need to enjoy the fruits of that spiritual friendship but find another person to act as your formal director. I have found on more than one occasion that a directee has grown so close in friendship that other issues entered in to block the best exercise of my director's discernment and guidance. None of this means that you should not become friends with a directee. But it does mean that the development of such a relationship may limit the original one, and it is your job as director to recognize this and bring it up for examination with your directee/friend.

LIVE IN THE LORD

The life of prayer and study enjoined upon you is unremitting. No vacations. No days off for good praying. You must live in the Lord in order to have him live in you. You must be open in your heart every moment for the movements of the Holy Spirit. This life of prayer and study will get in the way of other things and of other relationships. It will do this primarily by changing you. Old friends will feel uncomfortable with you even though you believe you are talking and acting as you always have. Your life will change. And you will pray over that. I can only say, "God help you," and know that he will.

LOVE YOURSELF

Finally, think of the sad and broken people you have known and dealt with in your life. Were you gentle and loving to them? Do you believe in your heart that they are loved and forgiven by Jesus even before they ask and accept that forgiveness? Have you not wanted to comfort and love them in the name of Christ? Then, in the name of Christ, be as gentle and loving to yourself day by day as you would be to those others. If you do not do this, then there is no comfort for your own directee when you "love your neighbor as yourself,"[1] for your too little love of your own redeemed self will translate into a too little love of your suffering directee. **One caveat here: You must not bless what Jesus came to redeem. Loving yourself or another does not mean denying that any sin exists there.** It does mean you must deal with each person in the constant knowledge that Jesus loves him or her exactly the way He loves you. You are being loved unconditionally every moment. "Go and do likewise."[2]

Endnotes

1. Matthew 19:19.

2. Luke 10:37.

A Spiritual Director's Soul

A spiritual director's soul cannot be a secret from the person being directed. The sharing of the director's life is basic to the scaffold of trust being built by the two of them. For this reason, I must at this point share at least a limited version of my own spiritual biography with you, the reader. Otherwise, how can you interpret my words? Much of the meaning between persons is found in the ***knowing*** between them. And so, I will try to show you something of who I am and what I am.

My soul grew up always knowing God. I don't know why. My earliest memories are filled with an awareness of his presence, even to the age of only two and a half years. This has been the blessing that has shaped my life and given me the courage to trust no matter what--and there have been plenty of "no matter whats!" This is also the blessing that has made me stand apart as one who is different--likable for the most part, I am told, but strange. I have felt the loneliness of this all my life; and that, too, has shaped me.

I remember the faith of my grandmother. She was the one who took me to church with her and did not think me quite so strange because I wanted to go. She was a person who believed in a simple way, but fully. When she died, I was 31 years old and knew I had lost the one person in my family who had an inkling of what my spirit was about.

My life is so full of mistakes. Isn't yours? If you think not, you surely are not considering it with an open eye. The biggest mistake I made was to believe that I could be a Christian quietly and alone. Many of my friends told me in later years when I had begun to change that they had thought I could sit in my study and read and write and pray with no need of anyone else. I suppose they believed that of me because I had believed it of myself. This is not true, friend. This is, in fact, a snare, and I have been caught in it. When I came out of my solitary tower, not everyone was pleased.

Some time in my 44th year I began to feel the call of my Lord Jesus so strongly that often tears would well up in my eyes. I began to let Him into the deepest parts of me and carry Him into every moment of my day. When this began to happen, I was transformed on the inside and changed in some way I was not aware of on the outside. Because I was not aware, I hurt and frightened people I loved. This is an enormous sadness for me.

What I did was to move into the community of Christians who felt the same kind of pull and fullness I did. We celebrated and mourned and studied and nurtured each other in a wonderful, loving way that was new to me. It was then that I began to learn what it means to be a member of the Body of Christ. It was then that I acquired a spiritual director and realized that I, too, through the years had been a spiritual companion for many others, limited though I now knew my understanding to have been. God had used me in this way all my life, and He was calling me through much study and hard experience to a fuller commitment now.

At this point, one of my directees gave me a gift of the full course of training in the School for Spiritual Directors at the Benedictine Abbey in Pecos, New Mexico. This generous, insightful gift has put me on a new course in the latter half of my life and brought me enormous joy. This small volume in your hands is an outgrowth of the years of directing and teaching of direction that have followed my affirmation in Pecos.

I have answered the call to write this book. I have done it in awe and, I pray, humility. ***And who am I, Lord, to write a book on spiritual direction? I don't know enough!*** There is a prayer happening here. Do you, reading friend, hear it?

Just now I have been in prayer with words much like these. I want a different assignment or else a lot more guidance! Here God is again, saying those same dreaded words, *"I've got something I want you to do. You're not going to like it. Later you will."* ***Right, Lord. Later. How much later, Lord?*** But I know it doesn't matter. I had to answer the call.

God calls to each of us, his children, in our "best" ear. I am a writer, and he calls me most clearly through my journaling, through the words I love so much and understand so well. Writing is my best ear.

One of my friends is a see-er, and God's call comes to her most clearly in pictures--a glimpse of the soul behind a face, something of God superimposed on the ordinary to reassure or to sanctify. She ***sees*** her call.

And, of course, many are feelers. They feel, they ***know***, in the gut with a surety they can find no way to defend. But they must defend it because they have felt the call and known it for what it is.

It is true that God calls us where we are, in the way we can perceive Him best, and in a glorious variety of specific ways. He calls to us in head, heart, and gut--as Lord, Lover, and Friend. We need to know and hear Him in as many of these ways as possible because He is himself of infinite variety. But, for each person, there is one way that is a surer path than the others. And here lies the calling of a spiritual director. Quite simply, the director walks and talks with the directee on that soul's Christian way and assists in searching out the paths through which God seeks to make known His call to that person.

What I know about writing this book is that the only unique treasure I have to offer is what I myself have learned about spiritual direction, the story of how I have learned it, and an ability to write it all down. My experience, like yours, friend, is unique. No other soul will ever have the same. And no other soul will ever tell it in the same way.

What is unique in me may be of use to you. And so, I offer what I am and what I know, answering the call. You, too, have a call to answer, else you would not be holding this book open in your hand and reading these words. If you are reading this book, if you have only picked it up to glance through the introduction, you are already in labor in the spiritual life.

Whether you are male or female, you are spiritually pregnant. May the Lord Jesus speak to you through these words. May new life come to birth in you. May you answer your call. And pray for me, friend.

Fleetwood Range
January, 1996

Annotated Bibliography

The Art of Spiritual Direction	113
Dreams	118
Healing--Mind and Body	121
Legal/Ethical Issues	123
C.S. Lewis	124
Living the Christian Faith	126
Personality Types	129
Prayer	131
Psychology and Christianity	133

The Art of Spiritual Direction

Barry, William A. and William J. Connolly. *The Practice of Spiritual Direction.* San Francisco: Harper , 1991.

Written by two Roman Catholic priests, this small volume is wonderfully hands-on and practical. Its emphasis is on the fact that a spiritual director is a facilitator, that the ultimate relationship being sought is between the directee and God, not between the directee and director. Highly recommended.

Edwards, Tilden. *Spiritual Friend: Reclaiming the Gift of Spiritual Direction.* New York/Ramsey: Paulist Press, 1980.

Edwards is an Episcopal priest and Director of the Shalem Institute for Spiritual Formation in Washington, D. C. Following the general themes of that Institute, this volume explores the background of spiritual direction and discusses the seeking of a spiritual friend. It also is quite useful in its discussion of the specific calling of a spiritual director and a practical program for the training of such a person. This book came to me early in my work as a spiritual director and gave excellent support and information.

Guenther, Margaret. *Holy Listening.* Cambridge and Boston: Cowley Publications, 1992.

Guenther is an Episcopal priest and Professor of Ascetical Theology and Director of the Center for Christian Spirituality at the General Theological Seminary. Her voice here is a woman's voice, not a feminist voice. This woman's voice tells truths about spiritual life and leading for, from, and among women that resonate strongly with my own experience. I have already said in the text of this volume that I am indebted to *Holy Listening* for much of what I have to say. Most particularly recommended here are the last two chapters, "Midwife to the Soul" and "Women and Spiritual Direction."

Hedberg, Thomas M. and Betsy Caprio. *A Code of Ethics for Spiritual Directors.* Pecos, NM: Dove Publications, 1992.

This booklet, which takes about 20 minutes to read, is an excellent overview of all aspects of spiritual direction, tightly focused on the ethics of such situations. It is clear, concise, thorough, and professional, yet it holds closely to the essential difference for this particular code of ethics--the difference that the relationship in spiritual direction is *three-way*, with God as the third party. This booklet is an absolute must for anyone who practices the art of spiritual direction.

Jones, Alan. *Exploring Spiritual Direction.* San Francisco: Harper & Row, 1982.

Alan Jones is dean of Grace Cathedral (Episcopal) in San Francisco. A reviewer in *The Living Church* says Jones' book shows this important ministry to be "basically good Christian common sense, rooted and grounded in the love of God in Christ, and enabled by the Holy Spirit to be effective." The emphasis is on companionship and community in the Christian pilgrimage. I find that I have marked on nearly every page. Highly recommended.

Kelsey, Morton T. *Adventure Inward.* Minneapolis: Augsburg, 1980.

Dr. Kelsey is a clergyman, spiritual director and counselor who has written many books in the area of spiritual guidance. Having been often told by others that secular journal-keeping instruction does not relate to their goal of Christian growth, he has distilled here his own 30-year experience in keeping a journal. The book is practical and specific, truly basic in its area. Highly recommended.

Kelsey, Morton T. *Caring.* New York/Ramsey: Paulist Press, 1981.

Dr. Kelsey is a clergyman, spiritual director and counselor who has written many books in the area of spiritual guidance. He says he became fascinated by the mystery and power of love and tried to work out his thoughts in a series of sermons over many years. Those sermons evolved into a set of lectures for a retreat entitled "How Can Christians Love One Another?" These lectures, in turn, became the basis of this book.

Kelsey, Morton T. *Companions on the Inner Way: The Art of Spiritual Guidance.* New York: Crossroad, 1989.

Dr. Kelsey is a clergyman, spiritual director and counselor who has written many books in the area of spiritual guidance. Based on long years of experience, this is a very personal sharing of his insights into the inner way and how we can be trained as guides on it. In the course of this volume, he goes into the history of spiritual guidance and discusses the nature and variety of religious experience.

Kunkel, Fritz. *Fritz Kunkel: Selected Writings.* Ed. John A. Sanford. New York: Paulist Press, 1984.

Fritz Kunkel was a German physician and psychotherapist, born at the end of the 19th century and trained in the early days of Freud, Adler, and Jung. He lived and worked in the United States from 1939 until his death in 1956, and had a profound influence on John Sanford, who edited this volume. This book is a core selection of Kunkel's writings and is included in this listing under spiritual direction as well as under psychology because he had much to say that is useful regarding the guiding and mentoring of others.

Linn, Dennis, Sheila Fabricant Linn, and Matthew Linn. *Good Goats: Healing our Image of God.* Mahwah/New York: Paulist Press, 1986.

This is a wonderful little book with whimsical color illustrations by Francisco Miranda. Its material is based on a retreat presentation given by the Linns for several years and includes a question and answer section that supports their earlier comments with the words of the Bible and the tradition of the Church. This simple, joyous presentation of the Good News of Jesus Christ can bring solace and comfort to the Christian who has lived in the shadow of an angry, fire-and-brimstone God. It can be especially useful in working with a directee who is struggling with a negative image of God.

May, Gerald G. *Care of Mind, Care of Spirit.* San Francisco: Harper & Row, 1982.

(Subtitle is "Psychiatric Dimensions of Spiritual Direction.") This is one of the few books I would consider essential to a spiritual director's library. Dr.

May is a board-certified psychiatrist and was, when he published this book, a faculty member in the field of spiritual formation for the Washington Theological Union and the Shalem Institute for Spiritual Formation in Washington, D. C.. He is, therefore, able to offer excellent practical help in the practice of spiritual direction, giving explanations and guidelines in many areas of the discipline. But all of this good, practical view of the inside of psychiatry is balanced against Dr. May's mystical knowledge of God. It is clear that he knows and loves his Lord. The gentle, encouraging way in which he speaks to the reader is a lesson in itself quite aside from the content. This book is a must!

May, Gerald G. *Simply Sane: The Spirituality of Mental Health.* New York: Crossroad, 1993.

Dr. May is a board-certified psychiatrist and was a full-time staff member of the Shalem Institute for Spiritual Formation in Washington, D. C., when this book was published. This book is a revision of Dr. May's first published book. He himself says that all his other writings are just footnotes to this work. His theme is that we don't need to be "fixed" but need, rather, to know that sanity exists within us. One reviewer says his voice here is "reflective, like a prayer."

Sellner, Edward C. *Mentoring: The Ministry of Spiritual Kinship.* Notre Dame, IN: Ave Maria Press, 1990.

Dr. Sellner is an Associate Professor of Pastoral Theology and Spirituality at the College of St. Catherine in St. Paul, Minnesota. In this book, rather than focusing on spiritual direction as a formal discipline, he takes a longer, broader view of spiritual friendship/mentoring. His emphasis is on the immense opportunity for growth that exists when there is spiritual closeness in a friendship. He says we mentor each other spiritually every day and need to be aware of the call to do so. There is a particularly good chapter on C. S. Lewis as a spiritual mentor.

Spiritual Life: A Quarterly of Contemporary Spirituality. Washington, D.C.: Washington Province of Discalced Carmelite Friars.

This is a small Catholic quarterly, normally some 60 pages in length. The articles pertain either directly or quite closely to the practice of spiritual direction. I find them quite good.

Tournier, Paul. *The Meaning of Persons.* New York: Harper & Brothers, 1957.

Dr. Tournier was a Swiss physician and psychologist. He believed that "the true view of man and his life is only to be found in the biblical perspective." He stressed the "fundamental importance of the personal relationship between doctor and patient on the one hand, and between God and man on the other." These themes led him into a developed understanding of humans as persons hiding behind personages, and he wrote his books from this standpoint. His work is an early example of ideas developed more thoroughly by Kelsey, Sanford and others. Writing in the 1950s in Switzerland, Dr. Tournier can sound dated to us at the end of the 20th century. Nevertheless, I recommend this book to beginning spiritual directors for the gentleness and compassion that glow in its pages. The Spirit is present here.

Dreams

There is an abundance of books on dreams available, and they cover a wide range of approaches and emphases. Since you are interested in dreams from the standpoint of finding Christ's leading within them, you will be most interested in what other Christians have had to say on this subject, though you should not ignore the opinions and experience of others who are experienced in this field.

Go to the Bible first and see again how God's people have been led, encouraged, and warned through their experience of dreams. Next, try to know something about an author's orientation before you spend money and time on a dream book. In the absence of any other information, I often choose a book on the basis of a commendatory foreword from an author I know and respect. Be wary of books that promise to tell you just how to interpret any given symbol or event or which do not reflect an awareness of divine action in human life. In light of these cautions, I have never found dream "dictionaries" to be of any real use to me, as it is ultimately the dreamer and no other person who can know what the symbol in his or her dream really means above and beyond its generally acknowledged references. Jung himself warned counselors strongly against giving too much weight to the arbitrary meaning of symbols in dreams.

The following is, I believe, a good "starter list."

Asper, Kathrin. *The Inner Child in Dreams*. Boston & London: Shambhala, 1992.

> Asper is a Jungian analyst who is strong and helpful in making the religious connections in dreams. This book examines the child in our dreams, using this material to gain understanding of our own childhood and see how that experience connects with essential patterns in our lives.

Clift, Jean Dalby and Wallace B. Clift. *Symbols of Transformation in Dreams*. New York: Crossroad, 1988.

The authors are a pastoral counselor and a clergyman who teaches religious studies. Their emphasis is on the healing inner transformations that are signaled in our dreams. They caution always to avoid confining the living dream symbol to any conventional meaning, urging instead an openness to the spiritual realities pushing us toward wholeness.

Savary, Louis M., Patricia H. Berne, and Strephon Kaplan Williams. *Dreams and Spiritual Growth: A Judeo-Christian Way of Dreamwork..* New York/Ramsey: Paulist Press, 1984.

Authored by a Ph.D. in sacred theology and spiritual growth, a clinical psychologist, and a Jungian analyst, this book holds close to orthodoxy, emphasizing relationship to God through dreamwork, and offering 37 different dreamwork techniques.

Sanford, John A. *Dreams: God's Forgotten Language.* New York: Crossroad, 1987.

Sanford is a clergyman and a Jungian analyst, widely known as a counselor, lecturer, and writer. He says this book is an attempt to "integrate a psychological understanding of dreams with a religious viewpoint." The emphasis is more on psychology than on religion, but he says in the preface that he is more concerned here with the "divine at work in the human soul" than with "elaborate creedal formulations."

Sanford, John A. *Dreams and Healing.* New York: Paulist Press, 1978.

The author is a clergyman and a Jungian analyst, widely known as a counselor, lecturer, and writer. This book contains a general introduction to the subject and then discusses in detail two series of dreams, one contributed by a young man and the other by a middle-aged woman. Neither subject was in therapy; the dreams discussed come out of quite ordinary lives and chronicle a process of inner healing in the dreamers.

Kelsey, Morton T. *Dreams: A Way to Listen to God.* New York/ Ramsey/ Toronto: Paulist Press, 1978.

Kelsey is a clergyman and a psychologist, widely known for his writing and teaching. He believes that the dreamer within us is the Holy Spirit, sent from God, and shows how this has been true through Bible stories, the experience of the early church, and in modern days. This book is strongly rooted in the religious understanding of our dreams.

Kelsey, Morton T. *God, Dreams, and Revelation.* Minneapolis: Augsburg Publishing House, 1974.

Kelsey is a clergyman and a psychologist, widely known for his writing and teaching. This book is a passionate argument for the position that the Bible is serious about dreams, that God does actually speak to us through them, and that they can bring religious insight to us. This can be a very good book to begin with if you question the significance and giftedness of our dreams.

Healing--Mind and Body

Linn, Dennis and Matthew Linn. *Healing Life's Hurts.* New York/ Ramsey: Paulist Press, 1978.

The Linn brothers, trained as Jesuits, write out of their active, dynamic ministry in the healing of memories. Their explanations and examples are accessible to the average reader, practical, and deeply encouraging. Their healing work is firmly rooted in the presence and action of Jesus Christ in our lives at all times and stages. If you have doubts about the discipline of the healing of memories, this book should dispel them. It should also set you on the road to your own personal healing.

Linn, Dennis, Sheila Fabricant Linn, and Matthew Linn. *Good Goats: Healing our Image of God.* Mahwah/New York: Paulist Press, 1994.

This is a wonderful little book with whimsical color illustrations by Francisco Miranda. Its material is based on a retreat presentation given by the Linns for several years and includes a question and answer section that supports their earlier comments with the words of the Bible and the tradition of the Church. This joyous presentation of the Good News of Jesus Christ can bring solace and comfort to the Christian who has lived in the shadow of an angry, fire-and-brimstone God.

Sanford, John A. *Dreams and Healing.* New York/Ramsey/Toronto: Paulist Press, 1978.

The author is a clergyman and a Jungian analyst, widely known as a counselor, lecturer, and writer. This book contains a general introduction to the subject and then discusses in detail two series of dreams, one contributed by a young man and the other by a middle-aged woman. Neither subject was in therapy; the dreams discussed come out of quite ordinary lives and chronicle a process of inner healing in the dreamers.

Sanford, John A. *Healing and Wholeness*. New York/Ramsey/ Toronto: Paulist Press, 1977.

The author is a clergyman and a Jungian analyst, widely known as a counselor, lecturer, and writer. He says here that "to be healthy means to become whole." This is the aspect of healing discussed in this book. Sanford ranges over many philosophies and religions, orthodox and other, discussing what humankind has learned about wholeness and its relation to physical and mental health.

Legal/Ethical Issues

Bullis, Ronald K. and Cynthia S. Mazur. *Legal Issues and Religious Counseling*. Louisville, KY: Westminster/John Knox Press, 1993.

Good, solid, brief (127 pages) overview of legal principles pertaining to religious counselors. Clear, concise discussion of specific cases. Charts with information specific to individual states. Good, useful, up-to-date reference for those whose religious profession includes a duty to do counseling. (This is not spiritual direction, but courts may not acknowledge that distinction, and clergy and licensed counselors will find it very useful.)

Kennedy, Eugene and Sara C. Charles. *On Becoming a Counselor: A Basic Guide for Nonprofessional Counselors*. New York: Crossroad, 1992 (New expanded edition).

Good discussions of problems commonly brought to nonprofessional counselors--e.g., physicians, undertakers, close friends. Useful information on how to listen, when to refer, what to watch for. Many cautions against going into the unconscious in any way. Reader must make the distinction between the deep unconscious holding serious emotional problems and the "safer" levels of the unconscious underlying daily living. (Again, this is <u>not</u> spiritual direction but is good general information for those in "helping" fields.)

Hedberg, T. M. and B. Caprio. *A Code of Ethics for Spiritual Directors*. Pecos, NM: Dove Publications, 1992.

This booklet, which takes about 20 minutes to read, is an excellent overview of all aspects of spiritual direction, tightly focused on the ethics of such situations. It is clear, concise, thorough, and professional, yet it holds closely to the essential difference for this particular code of ethics--the difference that the relationship in spiritual direction is "three-way," with God as the third party. This booklet is an absolute must for anyone who practices the art of spiritual direction.

C. S. Lewis

Lewis, C. S. *The Great Divorce.* New York: Macmillan, 1955.

In this fantasy, Lewis postulates a bus trip from Hell to the outer regions of Heaven. The damned don't have to go back, but we are shown why most of them prefer to. The "great divorce" of the title refers to George Macdonald's idea that it is not possible to have Heaven and keep a treasured little piece of Hell. The spiritual director will benefit from the ideas on illusion and reality expressed here.

Lewis, C. S. *A Grief Observed.* New York: Bantam, 1988.

This book is actually Lewis' journal, chronicling his desperate grief at the death of his wife. This story has become popular knowledge through the film "Shadowlands." Here in this journal is the daily struggle of a Christian soul to cling to God in the face of adversity.

Lewis, C. S. *Mere Christianity.* New York: Macmillan, 1978.

Subtitled, "What one must believe to be a Christian," this quiet little book is anything but a dull exposition of doctrine. In his usual incisive and often humorous style, Lewis sets out the long-accepted basic tenets of Christian orthodoxy. This is not an attempt to tell others what actions they should take in any given instance but to make clear on what understandings of Christian belief those actions must be based. His closing words are, "Look for yourself, and you will find in the long run only hatred, loneliness, despair, rage, ruin, and decay. But look for Christ and you will find Him, and with him everything else thrown in."

Lewis, C. S. *The Screwtape Letters.* New York: Macmillan, 1961.

This book consists of a series of letters from a senior devil in the "lowerarchy" of Hell to a junior tempter on earth. He advises on matters of human nature and temptation, explaining in wonderfully humorous and lucid language how the job is best done. In reviewing this book in *The New*

York Times Book Review, Anthony Burgess said, "Lewis is the ideal persuader for the half-convinced, for the good man who would like to be a Christian but finds his intellect getting in the way." It has much to say to a spiritual director of Christians.

Lewis, C. S. *The Chronicles of Narnia.* New York: Macmillan, 1950-1956.

Lewis regarded this series of books as "stories for children," and they are at least that. They are full of the stuff of classic children's adventure--fantasy, magic, talking animals, and high adventure. They are even conveniently written in chapters of about 10 pages each, just right for reading bedtime stories. On another level, however, they deal with the action of evil in a world created for good, with the sinful nature of even the noblest creatures in that world, and finally with the loving creator--expressed in a great lion--who gives even his own life to restore these creatures to his kingdom. I have never tired of rereading these stories. (They are arranged here in their order in the series rather than in alphabetical order.)

The Lion, the Witch, and the Wardrobe, 1950.
Prince Caspian, 1951.
The Voyage of the "Dawn Treader", 1952.
The Silver Chair, 1953.
The Horse and His Boy, 1954.
The Magician's Nephew, 1955.
The Last Battle, 1956.

Lewis, C. S. *Space Trilogy.* New York: MacMillan, 1965.

This trilogy is hopelessly dated as science fiction, but the stories are built on fruitful and deeply thought-provoking ideas. Beginning with an old but unfallen world (Mars), progressing to a new world (Venus) facing the first temptation of humankind, it concludes with an attempt to take over the earth by a group that sounds decidedly New Age. The theology in these adventure fantasies is clear and illuminating.

Out of the Silent Planet, 1965.
Perelandra, 1965.
That Hideous Strength, 1965.

Living the Christian Faith

Brand, Paul and Philip Yancey. *Fearfully & Wonderfully Made.* Grand Rapids, MI: Zondervan Publishing House, 1980.

Using St. Paul's analogy of the Church as the Body of Christ, this world famous surgeon and leprosy specialist shows how the intricacies of the human body express spiritual reality. Devotional and reflective, this view through the eyes of a celebrated physician who speaks with humility, faith, and awe can bear any number of readings and still offer new insights. Highly recommended.

Brand, Paul and Philip Yancey. *In His Image.* Grand Rapids, MI: Zondervan Publishing House, 1984.

See note above re Dr. Brand. This book extends the metaphor of the human body and the spiritual body. As fine a work as the first, *Fearfully & Wonderfully Made.*

Capon, Robert Farrar. *Parables of the Kingdom.* Grand Rapids, MI: Zonder- van Publishing House, 1985.

The author is an Episcopal priest and author of numerous books, all with an eccentric twist of humor. The subtitle of this one expresses that twist--"Jesus' Left-handed approach to a wrong-headed world." This is no ordinary commentary on the parables but a vigorous, salty, believing examination within their biblical context. Not for the faint-hearted!

Foster, Richard J. *Celebration of Discipline.* Rev. ed. San Francisco: Harper & Row, 1988.

This is a revised and updated version of the book first published in 1978. In it Richard Foster describes and explains the essential Christian disciplines in a simple, faith-filled manner that makes them accessible to all seekers. He covers meditation, prayer, fasting, study, simplicity, solitude, submission, service, confession, worship, guidance, and celebration. This is an essential resource for both director and directee. (See "Prayer" section for Foster's book, *Prayer.*)

Hurnard, Hannah. *Hinds' Feet on High Places.* Westwood, NJ: Barbour and Company, Inc., 1977.

This highly fanciful allegory teaches the lessons of accepting pain and evil and finding their transformation into the loving gifts of the faithful and loving God. Read it well and carefully, and you will know to whom it should be given.

Manning, Brennan. *Lion and Lamb.* Old Tappan, NJ: Chosen Books, 1986.

Subtitled "The relentless tenderness of Jesus," this book is itself relentless. Writing with humility, seriousness, and boldness, Manning carries the reader on a tidal wave of feeling in trying to express the reality of closeness with God. It can leave you shaking, but it cannot leave you untouched.

Manning, Brennan. *The Signature of Jesus.* Old Tappan, NJ: Chosen Books, 1988.

This is another powerfully felt book by Manning (see *Lion and Lamb* above). It is a plea to take the signature of Jesus--his cross--into the visible living of our lives day by day. He says, "Christians will look and act different from other people because they are different." This is a book of calling out--calling out the faithful and the committed, telling them to be different as Christ was different and to suffer as he did under the sign of his cross. Enormously powerful.

Sanford, John A. *The Kingdom Within.* Rev. ed. San Francisco: Harper & Row, 1987.

Sanford is a clergyman and a Jungian analyst, widely known as a counselor, lecturer, and writer. This book, originally published in 1970, is one of his earliest. In it, he invites the reader to move from the external meanings of Jesus' sayings to an additional internal, psychological parallel of them. The goal is to guide the seeker to a more conscious and creative life, the "kingdom within" of which Jesus speaks. This book can be an excellent first taste of what it might mean to live a fully conscious life under the lordship of Christ.

Personality Types

Brawner, Jim. *Connections*. Chicago: Moody Press, 1991.

This is a family-oriented book. It is meant to enhance the connections between parent and child by leading parents to a deeper understanding of each individual child. The explanatory means is the animal type system (Lion/Otter/Golden Retriever/Beaver) developed by John Trent and Gary Smalley. The material is fun, user-friendly, and Christian oriented.

Keirsey, David and Marilyn Bates. *Please Understand Me*. Del Mar, CA: Prometheus Nemesis Book Co., 1984.

Keirsey has adopted the typing system of Myers-Briggs, which is based in turn on Jung's theory of psychological types. The "Keirsey Temperament Sorter," offered in the first chapter, is a personality describer similar to the Myer-Briggs Temperament Indicator. It has the advantage of being shorter and more user-friendly than the MBTI. In addition, it can be legally used without additional permission and training from the developer. This book is helpful with most individuals because they can take the test and read the material with understanding on their own in addition to any explanation the director might give.

Michael, Chester P. *Prayer and Temperament*. Charlottesville, VA: The Open Door, Inc., 1984.

This book examines the relationship between human temperament and prayer and is organized around the different Meyers-Briggs personality types. The many different ways of praying described in this volume enhance one's understanding of the unique nature of each type in addition to giving invaluable material to offer in direction. The traditional spirituality and prayer disciplines discussed are Benedictine, Augustinian, Franciscan, Thomistic and Ignatian. (This book is also listed in the "Prayer" section of this bibliography.)

Myers, Isabel Briggs and Peter B. Myers. *Gifts Differing*. Palo Alto, CA: Consulting Psychologists Press, Inc., 1980.

The authors are the developers of the Myers-Briggs Type Indicator. This book is an explanation of the theory, effects, and implications of type as identified in that Indicator. Also included is a section on the dynamics of type development. This is a basic volume in studying the MBTI.

Prayer

Foster, Richard J. *Prayer: Finding the Heart's True Home.* San Francisco: Harper, 1982.

If you can have only one book on prayer, this is it. Richard Foster, best known for his excellent work, *Celebration of Discipline* (see the "Christian Living" section of this bibliography), has written a gentle, heartfelt celebration of prayer in this book. He works his way through 21 classic modes of prayer, divided into 3 groups--prayer seeking transformation, seeking intimacy, and seeking one's own ministry. His Quaker simplicity keeps this material warm and accessible on every page.

Fleming, David L. *The Spiritual Exercises of St. Ignatius: A Literal Translation and a Contemporary Reading.* St. Louis: Institute of Jesuit Sources, 1980.

There are many translations and interpretations of St. Ignatius' classic prayer exercise. This one is significant for the fact that it offers side-by-side versions--a literal translation and a contemporary reading of the incomplete notes left by Ignatius. This is a rigorous program if followed in its entirety. The modern reader will be surprised to find that the prayer methods of entering deeply into the Biblical scene were set forth so clearly over 400 years ago. Excellent material for an individual retreat.

Lawrence, Brother. *The Practice of the Presence of God* (rev. ed.). Orleans, MS: Paraclete Press, 1985.

Brother Lawrence was a 16th century Carmelite monk who worked in the kitchen and didn't really like it. He learned, thereby, "the secret of daily, moment by moment fellowship with God." It is a beautiful example of how a quiet life, faithfully offered at every moment, bears fruit beyond our wildest imagining. This particular edition includes biographical material and documents concerning Brother Lawrence.

Michael, Chester P. *Prayer and Temperatment.* Charlottesville, VA: The Open Door, Inc., 1984.

Although this book is organized around the different Meyers-Briggs personality types, it is valuable simply for its descriptions of many different ways of praying. The primary traditional divisions are Benedictine, Augustinian, Franciscan, Thomistic and Ignation spirituality and prayer. The prayer sugestions are both orthodox and creative. (This book is also listed in the "Personality Types" section of this bibliography.)

Psychology and Christianity

Hart, Archibald D. *Healing Adult Children of Divorce.* Ann Arbor, MI: Servant Publications, 1991.

Dr. Hart teaches psychology at the Fuller Theological Seminary in Pasadena, CA. This book captures the painful, frightening world of a child of divorce and carefully draws the conclusions concerning what that world means when the child comes to adulthood. There are several very helpful little quizzes in the text, and his comments are underpinned by a clearly-stated Christian faith. There are many books about adult children of divorce on the market, but this is by far the best I have found.

Jung, C. G. *Modern Man in Search of a Soul.* New York: Harcourt, Brace and Company, 1933.

This small volume is the most basic introduction to the thought of Carl Jung in his own words. It is not difficult reading on the whole, and an acquaintance with it is a useful grounding in conjunction with the works of Kunkel, Kelsey, and Sanford.

Kelsey, Morton T. *Christo-Psychology.* New York: Crossroad, 1984.

This volume has been described as a handbook that connects Christian seekers with Jungian techniques that may be new to them. Kelsey's practical advice on using these insights of analytical psychology will greatly assist any spiritual director, but especially the new one.

Kunkel, Fritz. *Fritz Kunkel: Selected writings* . Ed. John A. Sanford. New York: Paulist Press, 1984.

John Sanford has made the selections for this volume of Kunkel's writings. A reading of it will elucidate much of Sanford's work, as he is a devoted student of Kunkel's. Moreover, since Kunkel split with Jung in large part over the issue of the relationship of religion and psychology, it is instructive to see how this man carried Jung's theories of the psyche into the religious realm.

Miller, Alice. *Thou Shalt Not Be Aware: Society's Betrayal of the Child.* New York: New American Library, 1984.

This entire work is predicated on Miller's contention that abuse in childhood is covered up, forgotten, and denied by all concerned and that this denying of the problem is demanded by the Freudian theory of infantile sex drive. Further, the abuse of children--physical, sexual, and emotional--is so widespread that no spiritual director can afford to be unaware of its existence and the terrible consequences it brings. A soul that has experienced its father as an object of fear and danger will inevitably come reluctantly and untrustingly to God the Father. This book is an excellent grounding in this painful reality of so many people's lives, especially those of women.

Peck, M. Scott. *The Road Less Traveled.* New York: Simon and Schuster, 1978.

This enormously popular book needs no introduction, of course. However, two points are worth making concerning it. The first is that I have observed it to be an excellent "opener" instrument. Its sensible yet heartfelt simplicity and clarity of writing can help to spur serious spiritual journeying better than any other contemporary writing known to me. The second point is a caution that the book was written before Dr. Peck became a Christian, and I would want to tread carefully with my directee through his comments concerning the evolution of consciousness. In these pages, Peck equates the unconscious completely with God and also suggests that our spiritual evolution is intended to make gods of us ourselves. I believe a director would need to point out that the Christian lives into a more Godlike existence by the grace of God, but that he or she does not become God and cannot successfully hold this as a goal.

Sanford, John A. and George Lough. *What Men are Like.* NewYork/ Mahwah: Paulist Press, 1988.

The author is a clergyman and a Jungian analyst, widely known as a counselor, lecturer, and writer. Subtitled, "The psychology of men, for men and the women who live with them," this book is written in a popular, non-technical style, but it is steeped in Jungian psychological theory and will require careful attention for that reason. The authors trace the physical/psychological development of men, using anecdotes, history, and case histories to elucidate their ideas. This is another book that can be an excellent thought starter for both men and the women who live with them.

Schreiber, Flora Rheta. *Sybil.* New York: Warner Books, 1974.

This story is best known, perhaps, through the movie of the same name, but I recommend a careful reading of the book, especially in relation to Alice Miller's *Thou Shalt Not Be Aware.* I do not mean to suggest that a spiritual director has any business trying to treat a person with multiple personalities. I do know, however, that there is much to be learned by examining this phenomenon and also that it would be vital to have such information should you ever see signs of such a problem in a directee. Sybil is a fascinating, moving story of healing brought about primarily by love and trust, well worth reading on its own merits.

Smalley, Gary and John Trent. *The Hidden Value of a Man.* Colorado Springs: Focus on the Family Publishing, 1992

Smalley and Trent are authors and lecturers who have great gifts in the area of interpersonal relationships. The major themes in all their books are (1) the most basic differences between men and women in thinking and action, and (2) simple techniques for ensuring good communication between all persons. Their presentations, whether in person or in print, are entertaining, thought-provoking, and extremely helpful. This particular book discusses the positive power and impact a man can have within his family, giving guidance to both husband and wife on how to allow and celebrate that God-given power in a world which now often devalues men. In addition, I would recommend any of the Smalley/Trent books, tapes, and videos on personal relationships. They make their learnings wonderful fun!